Christmas 19

Richard Claydon
from Ernestine
Memphis, Tennessee

TOUCHED BY FIRE

(USAMHI)

TOUCHED BY FIRE

A Photographic Portrait of the Civil War

VOLUME ONE

★

William C. Davis EDITOR

William A. Frassanito PHOTOGRAPHIC CONSULTANT

A Project of The National Historical Society

LITTLE, BROWN AND COMPANY Boston Toronto

Second Printing

Library of Congress Cataloging in Publication Data
Main entry under title:

Touched by fire.

"A project of the National Historical Society."
Includes index.
1. United States—History—Civil War, 1861-1865—Pictorial works. I. Davis, William C., 1946- II. Frassanito, William A. III. National Historical Society.
E468.7.T68 1985 973.7'022'2 85-12967
ISBN 0-316-17661-3

KP

Designed by Patricia Girvin Dunbar

Published simultaneously in Canada by Little, Brown & Company (Canada) Limited

PRINTED IN THE UNITED STATES OF AMERICA

Contents

TOUCHED BY FIRE

Introduction

William C. Davis

"THE MEMORIES of our great war come down to us and will pass on to future generations with more accuracy and more truth-telling illustration than that of any previous struggle," Capt. A. J. Russell declared in 1882, and for that "the world is indebted to the photographic art and a few enterprising and earnest men." And so, indeed, the world is still indebted. No human epic prior to our own century is so richly preserved for us, in all the grandeur and honesty of the camera's eye, as the American Civil War.

More to the point, it is an epic of which we never tire, and never shall, and this, too, we owe largely to the visual legacy left for us by those who photographed the war. It is something that we can actually *see*, not in stilted and idealized prints and paintings, but in images that show the real faces and places, as they really looked, and often with the romantic veneer stripped away. Perhaps that is the hold that the faded old plates have for us; they reveal that only the trappings of warfare differed from then to now. The underlying drama and pain are the same, then and now, as in all conflicts, of all times.

It is the face of that war that this volume, and the one to follow, seek to portray. The photographers of the Civil War—chroniclers like Alexander Gardner, Timothy O'Sullivan, Jay D. Edwards, Russell, Mathew Brady's numerous assistants, and scores of others—were more than far-seeing when they covered the conflict. They were prolific. The fifteen hundred or more photographers who plied their craft from 1861 to 1865 probably produced in excess of one million images, the overwhelming majority of them portraits of individual soldiers. More amazing than their quantity is the number that survive today: at least several hundreds of thousands. And despite all the images that are well known and often seen, more continue to come to light for the first time, found in dusty attics, old albums, flea-market bazaars, or forgotten shelves in some library or archive. Even after more than a century, they still reemerge, like the phoenix, from the ashes of that war.

They allow us today to look at the Civil War in a way previously not possible—to see more of it than ever before, and in greater perspective. There are many histories of the conflict—too many, some would argue—and there are several good photographic works on it as well. It would be pointless to attempt to offer here simply more of the same. Rather, these two volumes approach the epic not chronologically, and not even in especially great depth of detail. That is all available elsewhere.

What they do seek to present is a flying overview of the war and its people from points of view rarely offered to the general public. These volumes will make no one an expert on campaigns and battles, leaders and strategy. But they will impart an understanding of some broader issues — issues like the nature of Civil War leadership and command, the spirit and story of the Civil War regiment and the men and boys who filled it, the role of the oft-forgotten navies, and the virtually continental scope of the conflict and its impact on the land. Special portfolios in each volume offer an in-depth look at the work of individual photographers who deserve better renown, and at the faces of the men whose war it was the most: Johnny Reb and Billy Yank. The texts, written by our foremost scholars of the war, are aimed at informing as well as entertaining.

And then there are the photographs, roughly five hundred of them in each volume, more than half appearing in print for the first time. They are what captivate us the most, and they have been selected both to expand upon and illuminate the text, as well as to offer a complete picture of America at war in its own house.

There is a special story of discovery about these images, for many of them had been forgotten and almost unknown until a few years ago, and a host of others have only just been brought out of three-quarters of a century of obscurity. Starting in the 1880s, a Massachusetts branch of a veterans' organization, the Military Order of the Loyal Legion of the United States, began to amass a collection of war photographs that eventually numbered more than forty thousand — the largest such collection in existence. But by the middle of this century, with all its original members gone, funds dwindling, and interest seeming to wane, the collection and the private museum housing it fell into neglect. Vandals broke in and stole some of the more than 120 bound volumes of images; dust and age began to take their toll on others. By the 1970s, the virtually forgotten collection seemingly had no future. But then it was, happily, turned over to the U.S. Army Military History Institute at Carlisle Barracks, Pennsylvania, and the work of preserving the treasure that remained began. And also, after years of being virtually "lost" to view, the images once again became available: scores — hundreds — of them are unique and available nowhere else. The great bulk of the photographs in these two volumes come to us from this milestone collection.

An even greater tale of discovery, of lost-and-found, lies behind several score of other images here presented. The first attempt at a comprehensive history of this kind appeared in 1911 when Francis T. Miller and the Review of Reviews Company published the ten-volume *Photographic History of the Civil War*. It was a monumental work — seriously flawed, to be sure, with inaccuracies and misidentified images, and a lot of the war's mythology still accepted as fact. But it has remained the benchmark against which all other photo histories are measured. Miller's researchers covered the nation looking for images, collecting thirty-five hundred that were published and probably two thousand more that never appeared. Many of those originals subsequently disappeared and, often being one-of-a-kind negatives, they have not since been available for viewing or publication except as mediocre reproductions made from Miller's 1911 edition.

But they were not lost — only in hiding. Miller failed to return some to their original owners; others he had purchased. And when he ran out of financing for the project and sold out to the Review of Reviews Company, the images became that firm's property. After the company went out of business, the two thousand or more remaining images stayed in the hands of the *Review*'s publisher, Albert Shaw, and spent the next several decades in a barn in New York and following Shaw's family through several moves. Finally they came to light again in 1982, and now, after seventy years in the dark, they can be seen again.

It is a magnificent collection. First, there are hundreds of images that, though collected, were never published by Miller. Better yet, there are several hundred more negatives made in 1911 of photos that Miller had borrowed, then returned. In all too many cases, those originals now cannot be found. But here we have perfect negatives made from them, negatives that allow a quality of reproduction far superior to the only other means of publishing them until now (copying from Miller's books). And the greatest treasure of all is surely the set of over sixty original glass-plate negatives made between 1862 and 1864 by the Baton Rouge photographer A. D. Lytle. Miller's agents bought these outright. So impressive are these photographs for their clarity and quality that a special chapter of this volume is devoted to Lytle and his work, with the images here reproduced taken directly from his original negatives. Happily, this whole collection of Shaw's, too, is now housed at the U.S. Army Military History Institute, resurrected from the dust.

There will be even more to see in the volume yet to come. The two presidents and the governments they led in trying to win the war, the role of industry in victory and defeat, and the part played by women and a surprising variety of ethnic groups await us. Forts, artillery, logistics, men of war, and a host of other broad subjects will appear, along with the portfolio depicting the face of Billy Yank, and a look at how the war has lasted through posterity. And all of it illustrated in the words of today, and the images of yesteryear.

It seems unlikely that we shall ever weary of looking backward through time to the people and events of those days long ago. The Civil War is too much a central part of our national consciousness. That we can still take the backward look is due in large part to the legion of intrepid men—and at least a couple of women—who waged their war with their cameras. Their work did not die with them. It goes on, as it does in these volumes, and it will continue so long as there are still forgotten attics to yield up fading treasures, so long as the world still holds people who yearn to look back to a time that is timeless.

Around the War

A portfolio of the America that for four years went a little mad and went to war with itself

It had been a quiet, peaceful land, untouched by war for nearly half a century, a land where a man could spend an afternoon quietly rowing or fishing in Virginia's James River. (USAMHI)

Still it was largely rural. Even near to state capitals like Annapolis, Maryland, with its nearby Naval Academy, there were fields of grain that fed its people. (USAMHI)

The moss-laden live oaks of Port Royal Island, South Carolina, spoke of a tranquil way of life that seemed destined to last forever. (USAMHI)

Natural wonders filled the landscape. From Umbrella Rock on Lookout Mountain, near Chattanooga, the daring viewer could see as far as he could imagine. (USAMHI)

The rugged slopes of Lookout Mountain had retained their unspoiled beauty for untold centuries. (USAMHI)

The Tennessee River flowing beneath it could just as easily have been any of a hundred peaceful streams that watered the land. (USAMHI)

Of cities there were plenty, many of them larger than the nation's capital at Washington, D.C. It was still in many ways a country city, its major industry government. (UR)

Only in recent decades had fine houses like those found in Boston and New York begun to appear on the capital's streets and avenues. Here on I Street, the homes of Sen. Stephen A. Douglas of Illinois and Vice-President John C. Breckinridge of Kentucky were just being completed in 1860, as the two vied with each other for the presidential nomination. (USAMHI)

Nearby Georgetown was hardly more than a port city on the C&O Canal . . . (USAMHI)

. . . while across the Potomac lay Alexandria, Virginia. (USAMHI)

Farther south sat Richmond, an old and stylish city, dominated by the Grecian capitol building. (USAMHI)

Just south of Richmond lay Petersburg, a major manufacturing and transportation center, one of the few in the otherwise industrially poor South. (USAMHI)

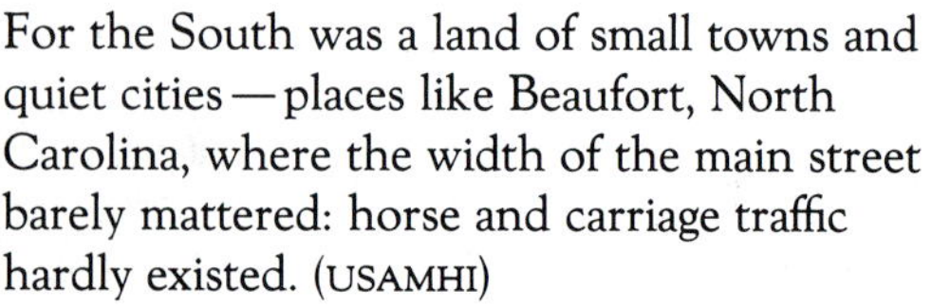

For the South was a land of small towns and quiet cities—places like Beaufort, North Carolina, where the width of the main street barely mattered: horse and carriage traffic hardly existed. (USAMHI)

Government touched people very little here, its main vestiges being a few public buildings like the customs house in Beaufort. (USAMHI)

It was a land of riverside backyards . . . (USAMHI)

. . . and peaceful public squares like the one in New Bern, North Carolina. Not since the last war with Britain, or perhaps the war with Mexico, had local militia trooped in these places for anything more than Sunday show. (USAMHI)

City markets like Savannah's bustled with produce and people. (USAMHI)

Saint Augustine, Florida, the oldest city on the continent, sat idly behind its seawall. (USAMHI)

And subtropical Key West, though little known and seldom visited, was as lush and beautiful as any island paradise of any time. (USAMHI)

The cities of the Southern interior were by turns sluggish and teeming. Atlanta's streets were always busy thanks to its major railroad and trading connections. (USAMHI)

The hotels of the Mississippi River towns saw the comings and goings of tens of thousands who traveled and traded up and down the mighty stream. (USAMHI)

And New Orleans — dominated by Saint Louis Cathedral, overlooking Jackson Square — was the jewel of the river, and of Deep South society. (USAMHI)

Rural though most of the South was, industry was on its way. Railroad trestles would bridge many of its streams. (USAMHI)

Small lines like the Wilmington & Goldsboro Railroad in North Carolina connected the seaports with the cities of the interior, and with the rest of the South. (USAMHI)

Major railroads like the Louisville & Nashville tied the cities of the region's interior in a network that, while thin and lacking in uniformity, could still move material—and men, if need be—with some speed from one state to another. The South's transportation was almost of an age to handle a war if necessary. (USAMHI)

Manufacturing was close to keeping pace. All across the region there were mills like Cloud's, near Alexandria, where water- or steam-power could grind grain and drive machines. An A. J. Russell image. (USAMHI)

Warehouses near every city were ready to store the produce of the South's few factories and many fields. (USAMHI)

The spiritual welfare of the region seemed to be in good hands, and certainly in good surroundings — such as historic Falls Church, near Washington. (USAMHI)

Indeed, churches were the most numerous public buildings in the South. (USAMHI)

Some were beautifully historic, like Alexandria's Christ Church, where Washington himself had been known to worship. (USAMHI)

There were even schools of religion, like Virginia's Fairfax Seminary — buildings large enough that they could be put to other uses if armies ever passed this way. (USAMHI)

Even some of the private homes of the South looked big enough to house more than families. (USAMHI)

None was better known than the Lee family home, Arlington House, on the heights of Virginia overlooking the Potomac and Washington. In 1860 its head of household was Col. Robert E. Lee, U.S. Army. (USAMHI)

Farther to the south, in the heart of Virginia, the home of a public man like John Minor Botts, near Culpeper, presided over a small domain of farmland big enough to quarter an army. (USAMHI)

Homes in places like Yorktown, Virginia, nestled quietly in groves of trees. (USAMHI)

Other mansions presided over untold ancestral acres. (USAMHI)

Down in North Carolina the homes looked almost somnolent, as if nothing could awaken them or their inhabitants from their peaceful existence. (USAMHI)

And then there were the plantation homes of the Deep South. Barnwell Plantation in South Carolina lay behind its avenue of undulating oaks in a setting emblematic of a way of life that its people had cherished for generations. (USAMHI)

It was a way of life that afforded to men and women of the aristocracy an indolence and tranquility hardly known elsewhere in the nation. (USAMHI)

Top left: But the Southern life-style was built upon an institution that had by 1860 grown odious in the eyes of the civilized world: slavery. One of Atlanta's many slave markets advertised "Auction & Negro Sales." So offensive was slavery to the people of the North—and even to many in the South—that for two generations it had been driving a wedge between the two sections. (USAMHI)

Top right: Southern politics had evolved around slavery, so that the region's greatest statesmen were, by definition, slavery's foremost advocates. None had been greater than John C. Calhoun. Though dead and in his tomb in Charleston by 1860, his spirit lived on. (USAMHI)

Slavery had created ardent foes. Of all who championed freedom for the blacks, none did so more vehemently or dramatically than John Brown of Kansas. His 1859 raid on the armory here at Harpers Ferry, Virginia, electrified the nation but failed to ignite the slave revolution he envisaged. (USAMHI)

The raid cost Brown his life, but though his hanged body lay "mouldering in the grave," his cause — if not his soul — did go marching on, firing antislavery sentiments throughout the north. (USAMHI)

Finally, and predictably, it was Charleston that could hold the peace no longer. The fine homes on the South Battery looked out on the harbor and the Federal forts it contained. On April 12, 1861, the firing began, and it would not stop for four years. (USAMHI)

And then the drums and the guns echoed across the continent, from the Atlantic to the Pacific, from the Ohio to the Gulf. This drum was to be one of the first, beaten by Federal soldiers as they marched through Baltimore to Washington on April 19, 1861, only to be mobbed by Southern sympathizers. The drum, like the spirit of the Union it served, was lost for a time. It would not be recovered without the drumming of the guns. (USAMHI)

The landscape began to change, subtly at first, profoundly in time. The peaceful streams still had their fishermen. But now the waterways were muddied by the hoof-prints of thousands of horses and millions of marching boots. The Hazel River in Virginia in the winter of 1863/64. (USAMHI)

Rivers once bridged by the iron rails saw their trestles destroyed to prevent an enemy's use, only to be rebuilt as the enemy advanced. Destruction and reconstruction were to be everywhere. (USAMHI)

Even historic landmarks were turned to war's uses, like this Indian mound in Alabama, now a Federal officer's headquarters. (USAMHI)

Places like Hilton Head Island, South Carolina, once peaceful plantation areas, became virtual cities of soldiers or, as here, headquarters of invading armies and blockading fleets. They would never be the same afterward. (USAMHI)

And any large building in the path of the armies was likely to be turned to another use: hospitalizing the thousands of wounded and the tens of thousands of sick. Like the innocence of the land itself, the men it raised were destined to die, in staggeringly tragic numbers. The Deaf and Dumb Asylum at Baton Rouge, now a Yankee hospital. (USAMHI)

Any rural inn or tavern might find itself unexpectedly used as office or headquarters by a Union or Confederate officer, and often by both in succession. The Alabama House at Stevenson was to be no exception. Only the colors of the uniforms changed; the sounds of the marching soldiers would be ever the same. (USAMHI)

Even religious institutions were not immune from being turned to war's uses, as the Fairfax Seminary found out. (USAMHI)

And the private homes of the South's gentry were soon enough commandeered by the invaders, as with the Aiken house in Virginia. (USAMHI)

No small farmhouse was safe from being surrounded by war. (USAMHI)

Places like the Globe Tavern near Petersburg would be swallowed by the armies. (USAMHI)

And the plantation homes of the South's wealthy and landed gentry were fair game for the uses of the military. Elliott's Plantation on Hilton Head. (USAMHI)

The stately home of John Seabrook on Edisto Island, South Carolina, played unwilling host to Yankees for years. (USAMHI)

And the park he built beside it afforded leisure now to his enemies. At times even the life-style of the conquered would be considered spoils of war. (USAMHI)

Top left: One by one the military installations of the South found themselves the targets of the Union's armies. Fort Oglethorpe was one of the few in Georgia to escape bombardment, but it could not prevent the Yankees from taking Savannah in the end. (USAMHI)

Top right: Places like the Oglethorpe Barracks, in Savannah, which once had been occupied by jubilant Confederates, echoed with Union voices once more. (USAMHI)

Bottom left: Military schools like Charleston's Citadel, which had trained officers for the Confederacy, fell once more to the Union as the city itself fell in 1865. (USAMHI)

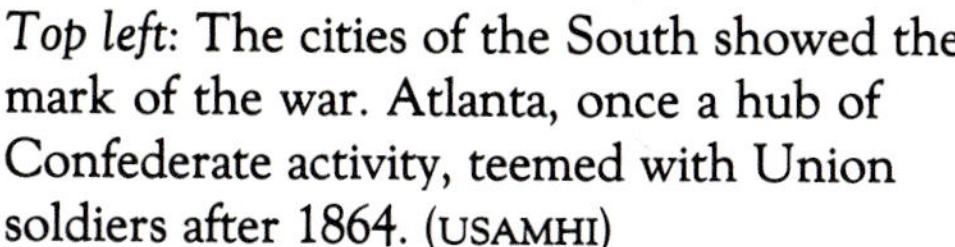

Top left: The cities of the South showed the mark of the war. Atlanta, once a hub of Confederate activity, teemed with Union soldiers after 1864. (USAMHI)

Top right: They were to be seen at every street corner. (USAMHI)

Bottom right: And carload after carload of them passed through on the rails, bound for the new war fronts deep within the Confederacy. (USAMHI)

Wherever the armies went, they left behind them new things on the land—especially their cemeteries and their hospitals. Sickel Hospital in northern Virginia stands amid the snow-covered countryside in January 1865, with the Fairfax Seminary on the distant horizon. (USAMHI)

As they passed, the armies brought vestiges of the military life with them, even to the minutiae of the soldier's well-ordered existence. Here at the Armory Square Hospital in Washington, D.C., a sign on the lawn repeats a military order that must have dated back to the Romans of antiquity: "KEEP OFF The Grass." (USAMHI)

Alas, the war showed on the children, as their dress took on a distinctly military look by war's end. These boys outside Richmond's Saint John's Church might well have been looking forward to the day when they would be old enough to go forth and fight with the Confederacy. Happily, they would not shed their blood in this conflict, but they and their progeny would have to live with its consequences for generations to come. (USAMHI)

Happily, too, both for their posterity as well as for the victors', there would be a record of the best and worst of the war for them to see, that they might never forget. Men like Mathew Brady knew that something profoundly historic was happening in America in the 1860s. He, and they, resolved not to let it pass unrecorded. (USAMHI)

And so, like this unidentified photographer, they took their cameras and their frail portable darkrooms out into the fields, to follow the armies, to follow America's destiny wherever it led, and to see and retain the image of a national epic. (USAMHI)

The Embattled Continent

★

Herman Hattaway

BETWEEN FRIDAY, APRIL 12, 1861, when Fort Sumter was fired upon and replied, and Monday, April 2, 1866, when President Andrew Johnson proclaimed that the "insurrection is at an end and . . . peace, order, tranquility, and civil authority now exist in and throughout the whole of the United States of America," 1,816 days elapsed. During that time the American Civil War was fought: 10,455 battle actions of one kind and degree or another, variously described then and later as campaigns, battles, engagements, combats, actions, assaults, skirmishes, operations, sieges, raids, expeditions, reconnaissances, scouts, affairs, occupations, and captures.

Some of the battles were mammoth, most were not, but size mattered little to the participants. To anyone being shot at, every engagement brought moments of sobering importance. One soldier wrote after a battle: "When I go home it will take me months to describe what I saw on that terrible field." The same might have been echoed by all the combatants.

Yet it is interesting to note that although actions occurred at the rate of six and one-half per day, the typical soldier experienced firefights only occasionally. Hard work and boredom were more the norm than fighting: soldiers spent much time getting ready for, getting to, picking up after, and refitting. "Time is tedious here," one Alabaman wrote to his wife, "we see little of what is going on; we are part of a grand army whose tents are pitched on the ridges all about us as far as we can see. . . . [But] what it is destined to do, is kept profoundly secret by the generals in command and we can only guess." Five days later he was in the Battle of Shiloh.

How long any particular battle might last varied considerably. Most of them climaxed in but a short time, typically a single day or even just a few hours or less. Some of the greatest battles stretched over two or three days, such as Chickamauga or Gettysburg. The week-long Seven Days Battles was atypical of the Civil War and proved to be something of a harbinger of World War II–style combat. The campaigns and sieges, on the other hand, dragged on long: Vicksburg was besieged for six weeks and Petersburg nine months.

All of these, along with Antietam — the bloodiest single day of the Civil War (indeed, the bloodiest single day in the entire American military experience) — make almost everyone's list of turning points. Yet battles, while sometimes cataclysmic, could never be totally decisive because Civil War armies lacked the power to annihilate each other. Technology, and developments in maneuverability and articulation of forces, rendered armies almost invulnerable to annihilation and almost always able to disengage, regroup, and fight again another day.

The distant killing power of Civil War–era fighting forces recently had been enhanced by the introduction of longer-range and more accurate rifled weaponry, and by engineering capabilities in the construction of entrenchments and forts. Some of the permanent works that were built, such as the fortifications encircling Washington, D.C., became so strong that one observer wryly opined that they ought to be renamed "fiftyfications." And as to field works, while in no previous American war had entrenchments been used extensively, in the Civil War they early became indispensable.

These things all tended to favor the side on the defensive. Indeed, one of the principal factors that made the war last as long as it did was the enormous inherent power and advantage enjoyed by defenders. The defense possessed roughly three times the strength of the offense. To overcome this, Civil War officers had learned the value of the "turning movement" from Winfield Scott during the Mexican War. But it proved difficult and rare during the Civil War ever to be able to reach an enemy rear with a large enough force to do the needed job.

So, even when the attacker "won" a battle, he usually lost more men than did the defender, because assaults were so costly. Indeed, any close engagement almost always dictated that both sides suffer immense casualties. The tactics used during the Civil War wasted untold numbers of lives. A Tennessean who had seen the results of the hopeless Confederate assault at Franklin exclaimed: "O, my God! What did we see! It was a great holocaust of death. Death had held high carnival. . . . The dead were piled the one on the other all over the ground. I never was so horrified and appalled in my life." Appalling casualties accompanied any period when troops were in close contact with the enemy — especially late in the war, during the 1864 campaigns, when assaults occurred frequently and the soldiers remained long exposed to losses from artillery fire, sniping, and skirmishing.

In this most costly of all American wars in terms of life — indeed, more costly than all of them combined through the Korean conflict — soldiers faced very unattractive odds. The precise numbers lost always have been uncertain and controversial. The best modern estimate lists 94,000 Confederates killed in battle or mortally wounded and 164,000 who died of disease, including between 26,000 and 31,000 Confederates who died in Northern prisons. The Federals lost 67,088 through battle deaths and another 43,012 to mortal wounds sustained in battle. There is precise information about other Federal deaths: 224,580 Yankees succumbed to disease, including 30,192 who died in prisons.

Total deaths in the Civil War amounted to well over 600,000: 365,026 Yankees (including 4,804 naval dead and others not specifically accounted for by the War Department) and 258,000 Rebels. About 18 percent of the slightly more than 2,000,000 individuals who served as Federals perished, while about 35 percent of the approximately 750,000 soldiers in the Rebel ranks died as result of the war. The common soldier faced unappetizing prospects. In the Union army, 1 out of approximately 30 men was killed in action; 1 of 46 died of wounds; 1 of 9 died of disease; 1 of 7 was wounded in action; 1 of 15 was captured or reported missing; 1 of 7 captured died in prison. For the Confederacy, 1 of every 19 white Southerners died because of the war.

Some 275,175 wounded Federal soldiers survived the conflict, as did at least 471,427 wounded Confederates. Many recovered fully, but huge numbers suffered permanent debilitation: about three-fourths of the 29,980 Union troops who underwent amputations survived; Confederate amputations were estimated at roughly 25,000.

And while the human damage wreaked by the war has to be regarded as vastly more significant than the other resultant physical damage, one is always shocked by the realities of the latter. The damage was lasting, even to this day: billions of dollars of losses in agriculture, industry, railroads, commerce, and education produced an almost cosmic jolt, from which the South simply never fully recovered.

The terrible mental strain of living through so obviously dangerous and damaging a war often induced in soldiers profoundly sobering thoughts. One Union seaman might have been speaking for all of his compatriots when he wrote:

How strange, peculiar, and indescribable are one's feelings when going into battle. There is a light-heartedness — a quickening of all the springs of life. There is a thrill in every nerve — an exhilaration of spirit — a tension of every fibre. You see every movement, hear every sound, and think not only of what is before you, but of home, of the loved ones there — of the possibility that you may never hold them again. Some men review their lives, and ask themselves if they have left anything undone which ought to have been done — if their lives have been complete.

Ambrose Bierce, who survived his soldiering to become famous later as a writer, vividly told about one of the war's more bizarre ironies: "Among [the dead left in the Cheat Mountain country of western Virginia] was a chap named Abbott. . . . He . . . was killed by being struck in the side by a nearly spent cannonshot that came rolling in among us. . . . It was a solid round-shot, evidently cast in some private foundry, whose proprietor . . . had put his 'imprint' upon it: it bore, in slightly sunken letters, the name 'Abbott.' "

The soldiers ranged in age from, as far as we know, thirteen to well over fifty, but the mass of them were quite young. One estimate holds that more than a hundred thousand boys in the war were under sixteen years of age. Drummer boys, which many regiments had, were below the age of thirteen. We have more statistics on the Federal army than on the Confederate. The average age of the Northerners was just under twenty-seven, but almost one-fourth of the group were twenty-one years of age or less. The Confederate army, even though it drafted men as old as fifty (whereas the Northern draft stopped at age forty-five), as a group was probably somewhat younger still.

The youth factor was almost as prevalent among the generals as it was among the lower officers and enlisted men. U. S. Grant was not quite thirty-nine when Sumter was fired upon; William Tecumseh Sherman was only forty-one. The average age in 1862 of the 132 Union men who became major generals was thirty-nine, and that of the 450 who became brigadiers was thirty-seven. For the Confederates, R. E. Lee was fifty-four, but his famed subordinate Stonewall Jackson was only thirty-seven. At the war's outset, the average age of the South's 8 full generals was forty-nine; that of the 17 lieutenant generals, forty-one; of the 72 major generals, thirty-seven; and of the 328 brigadiers, thirty-six.

But whether any given soldier was nearest in age to ten-year-old Johnny Clem, the Yankee "drummer boy of Shiloh," or Union brigadier general Galusha Pennypacker, who still was not quite old enough to vote at war's end, or seventy-nine-year-old Maj. Gen. John Wool, the Civil War was a great leveler that wiped away any such distinction and — as Confederate Stephen D. Lee, the war's youngest lieutenant general, put it — became the "sublime" experience of his life.

This was especially true for those who experienced a great battle, and the greatest battle of all was Gettysburg. No one could improve upon Bruce Catton's remarks as he described the scene on the third day — the famous Confederate attack on Cemetery Ridge: "The smoke lifted like a rising curtain, and all of the great amphitheater lay open at last, and the Yankee soldiers could look west all the way to the belt of trees on Seminary Ridge. They were old soldiers and had been in many battles, but what they saw took their breath away, and whether they had ten minutes or seventy-five years yet to live, they remembered it until they died."

The larger conflict was, as Walt Whitman called it, a "strange sad war." The people of the North and South seem certainly not to have hated each other at the outset, but the war brought out the worst in some individuals. Not long after the conflict's end, Confederate general Jubal Early wrote John C. Breckinridge to say that "I have got to that condition that I think I could scalp a Yankee woman and child without winking my eyes"; and on the other side, an ex-Massachusetts soldier proposed Southern genocide: "I would exterminate them root and branch." During the war soldiers might on occasion have declared their own unofficial truce to engage in swapping and visiting, or they might have shouted warnings to enemy personnel, maybe even refused to shoot at them. But when one Maryland woman saw Confederate captain Francis W. Dawson's horse fall with him astride, she remarked, "Thank God, one of those wicked Rebels has broken his neck."

The Federals eventually codified into military law the already manifest hesitancy of most soldiers in the ranks to fire on enemy sentries, as well as prohibitions against "wanton" violence, unauthorized destruction, pillage, sacking. The Confederates, too, proclaimed it "not admissable [*sic*] in civilized warfare to take a life with no other object than the destruction of life," and hence delineated a series of restrictions on the way land mines might be used, in addition to issuing orders forbidding the shooting of enemy soldiers while they were bathing. But such orders were issued because some troops had engaged in the activities in question. If some soldiers refrained from firing, for example, upon enemy personnel attending to calls of nature, others considered such to be good targets. Feelings hardened, and not at all unique was the Union cavalry colonel who in late 1863 assessed the situation in northern Virginia by saying: "I can clear this country with fire and sword, and no mortal can do it in any other way. The attempt to discriminate nicely between the just and unjust is fatal to our safety; every house is a vedette post, and every hill a picket and signal station."

But they were Americans — on both sides — and deep down, everyone knew it. Each side went to war certain of the wrongness of the other's cause, each feeling sure that God would grant them the victory, and thoroughly convinced that the enemy could fight neither well nor long. The magnitude and duration of the struggle changed all that. Those doing the actual fighting could not help but cherish respect for their foe. Thus could the Union's chief engineer, Joseph G. Totten, assess the Confederates' coastal defense in Georgia: "A compliment," he said, "should be paid to the officers and men who built these batteries on the Savannah. I do not believe that any but Yankees could have built them. By Yankees, of course, I mean Americans." Not only did the two sides come from the same culture, take pride in the same heritage, and speak the same language, thus making communication easy; they also had things of substance about which to communicate.

Some 3.5 million slaves were present within the Southern social structure, while in the antebellum North there were so few blacks that many whites had never even seen one. This was one of the principal factors that made the two sections truly different. And Southerners — rather much more, perhaps, than Northerners — learned some sobering truths about blacks as the war progressed. Brave blacks? Good soldiers? How could this be? Southerners had insisted that blacks were inferior, uncivilized, incapable; slavery was good for them — indeed, it was necessary for them. But the war provided opportunities, and the blacks in countless instances rose to the frequently heroic and often costly occasion and showed otherwise. There were at least 68,178 fatalities among the Union army's 178,895 black enlisted personnel and its 7,122 black officers. Many Southerners deeply respected the achievements of the "Sable Arm." In the end, the South, too, decided to put freed slaves into uniforms. The Civil War was going to dictate slavery's demise no matter how the contest turned out.

Great wars, such as the Civil War, tend to make some of their own conditions, almost as if they have a personality and a will. Thus was it impossible for poor Wilmer McLean to relocate his family to a place along the banks of Bull Run, near Manassas Junction, Virginia. When a shell came crashing through one of his windows during the war's first great land battle, McLean decided that he had had enough. So he moved the residence to a quiet country village in the southern part of the state: Appomattox Court House. There Lee's and Grant's forces clashed for the last time, and there Lee met Grant to surrender, on April 9, 1865, in the parlor of McLean's house.

The McLeans, of course, were not the only bystanders to be swept aside by events. Mrs. Judith Henry was killed during the First Battle of Bull Run while lying in bed; her house was totally demolished by artillery fire crossing from both sides. Huge numbers of spectators, however, had willingly flocked to see that first big battle. Many of them were injured in the stampede to the rear after the Federal lines broke. Later, it was not so much the norm for onlookers to try to get close to the fighting; many attempted instead to scurry away. Such, for example, was the case before Gettysburg. When Lee's men neared Harrisburg, Pennsylvania, one reporter described the scene as one of "perfect panic." Alarmed and excited people loaded with baggage packed the crowded trains. Perhaps fearing rape, "every woman in the place seemed anxious to leave," the reporter noted. But, unlike these Northerners, Southern women who fled invasion paths often encountered even greater hardships than those who stayed at home. And for many civilians, the war brought tragedy no matter what. One soldier wrote in his reminiscences about the burning houses and burning barns in Virginia: "Each time that we lighted our pipes that day, it was with the burning embers taken from the ruins of what a few hours before had been a happy home."

Whether innocent bystanders and victims or willing and sometimes vociferous participants, civilians truly shared in this war effort. Not least significant, to be sure, were the hundreds of thousands of citizens who only momentarily became soldiers. But note, too, the thousands of Negro slaves who were impressed into digging Southern entrenchments, so whites "could fight more and dig less." And think of civilian aides such as Governor Isham G. Harris of Tennessee, who served Albert Sidney Johnston at Shiloh, or fourteen-year-old Emma Samson, who once rode as a scout for Nathan Bedford Forrest (and years later was a darling of the United Confederate Veterans), or Capt. Sally Tompkins — one of the war's countless nurses and eventually the only woman to be commissioned in the Confederate army. Untold thousands of civilian workers labored directly in behalf of the war effort, such as the two thousand women who worked in the Confederate government's uniform factory in Richmond, and those who worked in the many other branch factories scattered from Virginia to Mississippi.

"We can't *help* it that the war after all *was fought* in Virginia," a sweet lady once said in defensive reaction to criticism of the too-frequent overemphasis by some students of the war in that state. Assuredly, many of the war's epochal events did occur in Virginia: 2,154 of the military actions — 20.6 percent of the total. But Tennessee, Missouri, Mississippi, and Arkansas were the next four leading theaters of the war by state, and together they were the scenes of 4,167 military actions. Every Confederate state had hundreds of engagements on its soil — except Florida, which had 168, and Texas, which had 90. There even were 88 in California (largely against Indians), 75 in the New Mexican Territory, and even 1 in Vermont, when a small band of Confederates thrust from Canada to rob banks at Saint Albans and there ensued a firefight between them and a local militia.

Veritably, the war affected in some way almost all of the embattled continent. The conflict was far from exclusively fought — nor decided — in that epochal battle of Gettysburg where the South's forces were led by Virginia's great hero, R. E. Lee. The hills around Vicksburg and Chattanooga were as fateful as those in Pennsylvania.

Americans know that today, and they visit the Civil War battlefields by the millions every year. Gettysburg, Fredericksburg-Spotsylvania, Chickamauga, Chattanooga, Vicksburg, Kennesaw Mountain, Harpers Ferry, Petersburg, Fort Donelson, Antietam, Richmond, Tupelo, Fort Pulaski, Appomattox, Shiloh, Fort Sumter, Stones River, and Brice's Cross Roads attract a constant stream of visitors. But so, too, might one be inspired or learn something worthwhile on visits to the engagement sites at Pigeon's Ranch, New Mexico; Honey Hill, South Carolina; and Amelia Springs, Virginia; and much edification might await those who have not yet been to the skirmish sites of Turkeytown, Alabama; Pea Vine Ridge, Georgia; Crab Orchard and Barren Mound, Kentucky; Pest House, Louisiana; Klapsford, Missouri; Moccasin Swamp, North Carolina; Whippy Swamp, South Carolina; and Shanghai, West Virginia.

The Civil War was the great American Iliad, the ordeal of the Union, the great crimson gash in American history. The names of its battles endure, and will endure perhaps forever. The "awed stillness" that so impressed Joshua Chamberlain at Appomattox has been perceived and felt anew, year after year, by the countless numbers of pilgrims who have trekked to these scenes of former struggle.

The war spread all over the land, even before the fighting started. Here in Pensacola, Florida, the once tranquil Gulf Coast began to see and hear guns. (USAMHI)

Sand batteries like this one aimed their guns at Florida's Fort Pickens, ready to open fire when ordered, and ready to plunge the nation into war. A J. D. Edwards image. (USAMHI)

Though they rarely fired in anger, they had scarred the land already. (SHC)

Elsewhere, guns did fire in anger. In northern Virginia, in July 1861, the first armies met near Centreville. (USAMHI)

On July 18, 1861, they clashed near Blackburn's Ford on Bull Run. (USAMHI)

Once peaceful farmhouses became generals' headquarters as the battle that many believed would begin and end the war was fought in the nearby fields. (USAMHI)

But what that first Battle of Bull Run began would not be stilled quickly, and the Virginia landscape that it left ravaged was only to be the first of many rural places injured by war. (USAMHI)

Quickly the war spread south and west. In April 1862, Fort Pulaski, Georgia, which had never fired a shot in America's previous wars, first heard the guns as American fought American. Federals bombarded it into submission and, in the process, demonstrated that the era of the masonry fortification was over. (USAMHI)

And out west in Tennessee, Federals demonstrated that the Confederates were not as invincible as they thought. At Shiloh, these and other guns drove back a Rebel attack and helped save western Tennessee for the Union. (USAMHI)

But always the war seemed to capture the most attention in Virginia. Historic places from the days of the Revolution echoed once again to the booted heels of marching men. Lafayette's headquarters at Yorktown would play host to Yankee foot soldiers now. (USAMHI)

While along the banks of the York River, shore batteries bristled with guns planted by Confederate defenders. (USAMHI)

This Rebel water battery at Gloucester Point mounted fifteen heavy guns, ready to strike any enemy fleet. When Yorktown fell, so did they. (USAMHI)

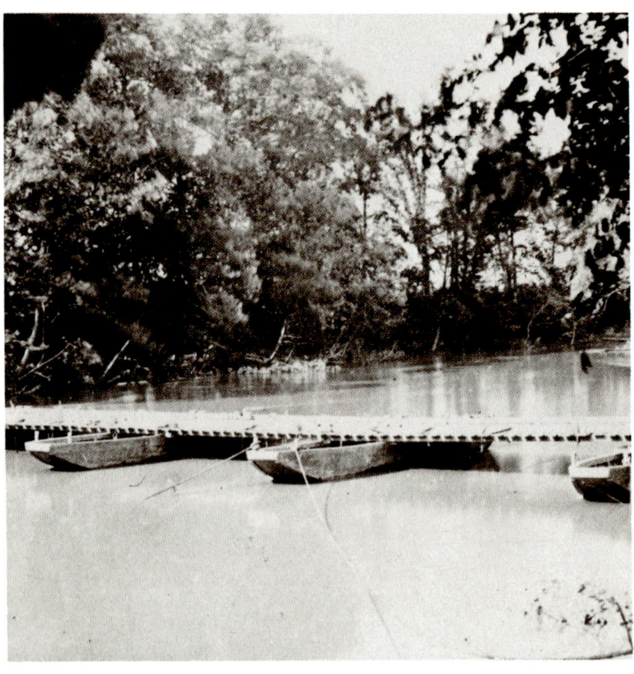

In the campaign for the Virginia Peninsula, peaceful streams like the Pamunkey became major crossing places for the advancing Union army. (USAMHI)

And at places like Cumberland Landing, on the Pamunkey, tens of thousands of men from the Army of the Potomac rested briefly before going (so they thought) "on to Richmond." (USAMHI)

The Yankees thronged every dock and wharf on the Pamunkey — like White House Landing, shown here with the river full of craft in the distance. (USAMHI)

In what would be called the Seven Days Battles before Richmond, several little-known places like Mechanicsville became suddenly nationally important as Lee and McClellan battled for the Confederate capital. (USAMHI)

Though McClellan was unsuccessful, his fellow general John Pope was no more fortunate as he battled Lee on the old Bull Run battleground. The Confederates had fortified here at Manassas Junction before abandoning their works. (USAMHI)

When next the armies met it was on South Mountain, as Lee invaded Maryland. It was in this field that a Yankee corps commander, Jesse Reno, was mortally wounded. (USAMHI)

And then they were on to Antietam, the bloodiest single day of the Civil War. This image by Alexander Gardner or James Gibson looks across the famous Burnside Bridge toward the Union positions. Across this bridge thousands of Yankees attacked, running headlong into Rebel guns. (LC)

Top left: Bloody assaults came in December, too, when Ambrose Burnside sent brigade after brigade against this stone wall on Marye's Heights at Fredericksburg. Rebels firing from behind it devastated their foes. (USAMHI)

Top right: The Marye house itself showed the effects of the combat, and of the May 1863 battle fought on the same ground. Almost every pane of glass in the house was broken, and its brick walls were pocked by cannonballs. (USAMHI)

Bottom left: Meanwhile, out in the West, the Union juggernaut was moving more swiftly. Nashville was securely in Yankee hands, its wharves teeming with transport shipping to supply the Federals. (USAMHI)

In the spring of 1863, the campaigns began everywhere. In the fields and woods around Dowdall's Tavern, near Chancellorsville, the two armies in Virginia met yet again, in the greatest victory of Lee's career. (USAMHI)

While Lee defeated his opponent at Chancellorsville, his subordinates were holding their own in yet another fight on the Fredericksburg battleground. This A. J. Russell image looks across the Rappahannock toward the city, from a Union battery. (USAMHI)

The casualties were terrible in the fighting. The war would bring thousands of headboards to Fredericksburg. (USAMHI)

And much of the city itself was left in ruins. (USAMHI)

Then, less than a month after Chancellorsville, came the greatest battle of the war, the three days at Gettysburg. This is the view that many of Lee's Confederates saw when they first took the town on July 1, 1863. (KA)

Even citizens turned out to defend their town, among them old John Burns, veteran of the war of 1812, shown here on his porch with an unidentified bystander. (USAMHI)

The fighting was ferocious as the Rebels tried to penetrate the Yankee line on Cemetery Hill, near this gatehouse to Evergreen Cemetery. (USAMHI)

Most crucial of all in the first two days of fighting was the contest for Little Round Top. Alexander Gardner's image made a few days after the battle shows some of the bloated dead still unburied. (USAMHI)

Indeed, the dead were everywhere. (USAMHI)

Corpses lay amid the rock outcroppings. (USAMHI)

And in the fields. (USAMHI)

It required a major humanitarian volunteer effort to clean the town and bury the dead once the battle was done. (USAMHI)

And the thousands of wounded had to be cared for at field hospitals like this one operated by the II Corps. Gettysburg had been scarred by war forever. (USAMHI)

At virtually the same time, the war for the Mississippi was raging, as U. S. Grant tried to take his greatest prize, Vicksburg. On the way he suffered setbacks, as here at Chickasaw Bluffs. . . . (USAMHI)

But in the end the prize was Grant's, and on July 4, 1863, Vicksburg surrendered. Sometime thereafter the Yankee gunboat ram *Vindicator* posed for the camera with the city in the background, symbolic of the might of the Union. (WLM)

The conflict moved on into north Georgia in the fall, with the Union suffering its most complete defeat of the war along Chickamauga Creek, not far from Lee & Gordon's Mills. Almost a whole army was put to rout. (LC)

The vanquished were driven back to Chattanooga, in the shadow of giant Lookout Mountain. (USAMHI)

Top left: Here, with bridge construction under way along the Tennessee River, the Federals built up their fortifications to resist the besieging Confederates. (USAMHI)

Bottom left: And here, on Missionary Ridge, the Confederates established their lines, only to be driven off in one of the grandest infantry assaults of the war. The Union was on the move again. (USAMHI)

Bottom right: Elsewhere in Tennessee, the Yankees reclaimed Cumberland Gap, vital link between the east and west sides of the Appalachians. Here, in a previously unpublished print, Union camps dot the hillsides that shelter a cavalry unit. (KHS)

And then the Federals resisted a Confederate attempt to retake Knoxville, where the Rebels spent themselves in bloody attacks at Fort Sanders, shown here after the battle as a lone Yankee surveys the scene of the fighting. Everywhere the armies went on the continent, they seemed to leave the marks of their passing in the cleared fields and ravaged forests. (USAMHI)

Then came 1864 and the opening of new, major campaigns all across the continent. Once more the Army of the Potomac marched across the Rapidan and into the Wilderness near Chancellorsville, there to meet and fight Lee. (USAMHI)

A host of new places, like the unassuming Todd's Tavern, saw the coming of the armies, locked now in a death grip that would not loose until the end. (USAMHI)

Grant estabished huge supply bases on the Virginia rivers to succor his advancing army — bases like this one at Belle Plain, photographed by Russell on May 18, 1864. (USAMHI)

Bottom left: Every stream and river had to be bridged. The Pamunkey River in May 1864. (USAMHI)

Bottom right: The pontoon bridges crossed everywhere as the armies literally took their bridges with them. (USAMHI)

Finally the armies locked in the siege of Petersburg, and the Confederates clung to formidable earthwork defenses like these just recently captured. (USAMHI)

The Virginia city was literally ringed with trenches and fortifications. For as far as the eye could see, they snaked across the landscape. (USAMHI)

Even cruel weather, which could destroy bridges, could not deter him from his determination to have his quarry. (USAMHI)

His batteries surrounded the beleaguered Rebels. (USAMHI)

Everywhere they looked, Lee's Confederates saw an enemy determinedly staring back at them. (USAMHI)

While the ten-month siege wore on, Grant's other armies advanced into the heart of the Confederacy. Units like this Missouri artillery battery joined with Sherman as he drove deep into Georgia. (USAMHI)

From one defensive position to another, Sherman drove the Rebels before him, marching over their defenses, as here at the Etowah River bridge, shown in a George Barnard image. (LC)

At last Sherman took Atlanta, and his officers could pose in front of the headquarters of their foe, Gen. John B. Hood, with the Stars and Stripes proudly draped from its balcony. (USAMHI)

Hood's last gasp would be his attempt in late fall of 1864 to reclaim middle Tennessee — an effort that culminated in the debacle at Nashville, where he almost saw his army destroyed. The state capitol looks out over the scene of some of the war's bitterest fighting. (NA)

Even out in the Far West, the Federals were on the march, reclaiming Brownsville, Texas, and forcing the Confederates to evacuate across the Rio Grande on pontoon bridges like this. (USAMHI)

The Yankee drives could not be stopped. Sherman pushed on from Atlanta to the sea, and then marched northward through the Carolinas. Columbia fell to him, and its fall left much of the city devastated, like the state armory shown here. A lounging Union photographer sits in the foreground beside his wagon. (USAMHI)

And the blockade grew ever tighter as one after another of the South's port cities fell—and with them the forts that guarded them, like Fort Fisher, North Carolina. (USAMHI)

Its interior ruin spoke for the state of the Confederacy as a whole as it approached its final days of nationhood. (USAMHI)

In the end, Petersburg, too, had to fall, leaving the miles and miles of muddy trenches and earthworks behind as Lee's Confederates desperately tried to escape Grant's encircling minions. (USAMHI)

Lee tried to burn High Bridge, over the Appomattox River, behind him to stop Grant, but it did not work. It was only an issue of days and hours now. (USAMHI)

And then, finally, it was done. The embattled continent came to peace once more as Grant and Lee met to accept the Confederate's surrender here at the McLean house in the town known as Appomattox Court House, while the other Rebel armies carried on for a few weeks more before they, too, succumbed. The land they left behind them, like its people, would never again be the same. (USAMHI)

The Men in the Ranks

★

Perry D. Jamieson

WHEN THE WAR BEGAN, old army veterans were wryly amused by the enthusiasm and dashing uniforms of the volunteer regiments. The men of the Sixteenth New York wore straw skimmers, until they learned on the Virginia Peninsula in 1862 that their fancy white hats made excellent targets. There were colorful zouave regiments with baggy trousers and Turkish fezzes—units such as the Fifth New York, which took devastating losses at Second Bull Run, and the Ninth New York, which fought stubbornly at Antietam. The Thirteenth Pennsylvania Reserves came from the "wildcat district" of Forest, Elk, and McKean counties, and most of its members were lumbermen, who reported to the regiment in red flannel shirts. One soldier decorated his hat with a piece of deer fur, his comrades copied him, and the unit became famous as the Pennsylvania Bucktails.

Other units were conspicuous for their weapons or mascots. The Twelfth New Jersey fired "buck and ball" from their 69-caliber smoothbores, while Berdan's Sharpshooters boasted Sharps rifles. Col. Richard H. Rush's Sixth Pennsylvania Cavalry was known throughout the Army of the Potomac as Rush's Lancers. Maj. Gen. George B. McClellan suggested that the regiment be armed with lances, and its officers voted to accept the idea. The troopers received nine-foot Austrian lances, with eleven-inch, three-edged blades and scarlet streamers. The Eighth Wisconsin was called the Eagle Regiment: its mascot was Old Abe, a bald eagle. Perched on a stand near the regiment's flag, the bird of prey accompanied the Eighth on the march and into battle. Dozens of other regiments, now forgotten, were famous in their day.

Sometimes an entire brigade gained distinction. Brig. Gen. John Gibbon's Black Hat Brigade from the Old Northwest wore high-crowned black hats known in the old army as Hardee or Jeff Davis hats. The brigade was made up of three Wisconsin regiments and the Nineteenth Indiana, joined later by the Twenty-fourth Michigan. The brigade's performance at South Mountain won it an even more famous nickname: the Iron Brigade. The unit's fight on the first day at Gettysburg was among the finest brigade actions of the war. The Irish Brigade, raised by Thomas F. Meagher in New York City, consistently encountered the Confederates in difficult positions, such as the Bloody Lane at Antietam and Marye's Heights at Fredericksburg. One Confederate officer remembered the brigade's courageous advance at Fredericksburg: "In the foremost line we distinguished the green flag with the golden harp of old Ireland, and we know it to be Meagher's Irish brigade." At Gettysburg, Fr. William Corby offered general absolution to the brigade before it entered the maelstrom of the second day's battle. "That general absolution was intended for all," Father Corby later wrote, "not only for our brigade, but for all, North or South, who were susceptible for it and who were about to appear before their Judge." In the western theater, Brig. Gen. William B. Hazen's brigade was remembered for its stubborn combats at Stones River and Chickamauga, while Brig. Gen. John C. Starkweather's brigade suffered heavily at Perryville and Chickamauga.

Southerners had their famous units as well. Five Virginia regiments formed the brigade known as Stonewall, which earned that nickname for itself, and its commander, at First Manassas. The 1862 campaigns wore down this outstanding brigade, until at Sharpsburg it had only 250 men in its ranks; and in that battle it lost another 11 killed and 77 wounded. Thomas J. ("Stonewall") Jackson's staff officer, Henry Kyd Douglas, quoted some of Jackson's dying words: "They are a noble set of men. The name of Stonewall belongs to that brigade, not to me." Hood's Texas Brigade, commanded by Kentucky-born Brig. Gen. John Bell Hood, stormed across battlefields of both theaters of the war. It was the only unit to break the Union line at Gaines' Mill, and suffered fearful losses at Second Manassas, Sharpsburg, and Gettysburg. In the famous "General Lee to the rear" episode during the Battle of the Wilderness, the soldiers of the Texas Brigade turned Traveller and his irreplaceable rider to the rear when Lee sought to lead a charge personally, before the brigade would go forward. During the Petersburg campaign, General Lee once observed: "The Texas brigade is always ready." Western soldiers knew the First Kentucky Brigade as the Orphan Brigade—its men fought the war isolated from their homes in the Upper South. After the brigade's hopeless charge at Murfreesboro, Maj. Gen. John C. Breckinridge lamented: "My poor Orphan Brigade! They have cut it to pieces!"

The men of these brigades marched in columns, long streams of soldiers that filled the back roads of Mississippi, Tennessee, and Virginia. The standard tactical manuals of the day, William J. Hardee's *Rifle and Light Infantry Tactics* and Silas Casey's *Infantry Tactics*, called for the men to march at a route step of 110 paces a minute. During his famous Shenandoah Valley campaign, Stonewall Jackson insisted on a regimen that alternated precisely fifty minutes of marching at route step with exactly ten minutes of rest. Even at a slower pace, marching was tedious work. One Confederate wrote of a march during the Second Manassas campaign: "There was no mood for speech, nor breath to spare if there had been—only the shuffling tramp of the marching feet, the steady rumbling of wheels, the creak and rattle and clank of harness and accouterment, with an occasional order, uttered under the breath and always the same: 'Close up! close up men!'"

Stunning marches punctuated many campaigns. Jackson's "foot cavalry" made astonishing marches during the Shenandoah Valley, Second Manassas, and Chancellorsville campaigns. Maj. Gen. William T. Sherman's men completed their famous advance from Atlanta to Savannah in twenty-five days. At the opening of the Shenandoah Valley campaign of 1864, Lt. Gen. Jubal A. Early pressed his veterans to cover more than eighty miles in four days.

A poor march also might influence a battle or campaign. The men of Brig. Gen. Lew Wallace's division spent the afternoon and evening of April 6, 1862, in a disjointed march and countermarch of about thirteen miles, and arrived across Snake Creek too late to help their comrades in the desperate first day's fighting at Shiloh. Stonewall Jackson prodded his men to brilliant marches during his Shenandoah Valley campaign, but during the Seven Days Battles that immediately followed, confusion and tardiness characterized the movements of his command, while the Confederates missed a series of opportunities to strike a decisive blow against the Army of the Potomac. A mistake in marching orders delayed by several hours the arrival of Maj. Gen. William F. Smith's corps at Cold Harbor on

June 1, 1864. A staff officer explained to army commander George G. Meade that Smith had little ammunition, no wagons, and his corps was in a vulnerable position. "Then why in hell," Meade asked, "did he come at all?"

Moving a mass of soldiers from a marching column into a fighting line was a complicated business, requiring that officers master detailed drill-book instructions, such as those describing the four different "modes of passing from column at half distance, into line of battle." Brig. Gen. John Beatty, a volunteer soldier, complained that he spent the first summer of the war struggling to understand his drill manual. "The words conveyed no idea to my mind," he admitted, "and the movements described were utterly beyond my comprehension." Shortly after the war, one veteran commented that he "never saw a full company execute the facings" according to Casey's *Tactics* "without making mistakes." Yet Beatty and thousands of other officers studied their tactical manuals until they mastered them, and their men got into their places, if not always according to the book.

Regiments deployed into line of battle with a regimental flag, or perhaps the national colors, prominently displayed in their front rank. Civil War soldiers invested great emotion in these banners. In June 1863 a Confederate officer wrote proudly that his regiment had marched into Pennsylvania with its "red battle flag inscribed all over with the names of our victories." Three days after the bloodbath at Antietam, a New York infantryman recounted: "Our color guards were cut down almost to a man and Kimball, our hot headed Lieut. Colonel, finally seized the flag himself and wrapped it round him. Strange to say, he was uninjured." At Murfreesboro, the color sergeant of the Twenty-fifth Tennessee ripped his flag from its staff and hid it in his uniform to prevent it from being captured. This enterprising sergeant was taken prisoner, escaped, and proudly returned to his unit, with its flag. The officers of the Eleventh North Carolina burned their flag rather than surrender it to the Yankees at Appomattox.

The colors aroused unit pride, and they also served a practical function in battle. This was a black-powder war. A regiment deploying into line, advancing into a woodlot, and opening fire soon engulfed itself in an enormous cloud of white smoke. On a warm, calm day in heavy woods, the cloud would linger over the firing line, and it would become more dense as neighboring units added their volleys. The roar of artillery and shoulder arms drowned the voices of officers and the sound of drums, and enemy fire often cut down mounted officers. In the reigning smoke and confusion, many times the infantryman's best assurance of his regiment's location was a quick glimpse of the colors waving in the white cloud of battle.

The number of flags in an area suggested how many regiments were there. This maxim was illustrated by a postwar anecdote about Stonewall Jackson at Sharpsburg. Jackson, wanting to launch a counterattack, ordered a North Carolina soldier to climb a tree that commanded the Union ground beyond the East Woods. The general told the man to count the Federal flags in that sector, and when the Tarheel had reached thirty-nine, Jackson called him down. Stonewall had learned that there were too many Yankees, and he canceled the assault. General Lee used the same tactic in 1864 at Petersburg, during the Battle of the Crater. He had Col. W. H. Palmer count Union battle flags, as a measure of the extent of the break in the Confederate line.

The movement of the colors usually told the course of a battle. The flags often were at the forefront of a successful attack, such as the Federal advance up Missionary Ridge at Chattanooga. William B. Hazen reported of his brigade in that charge: "Not much regard to lines could be observed, but the strong men, commanders and color bearers, took the lead in each case, forming the apex of a triangular column of men." A concentration of flags might also mark a defeat. When the Confederates were repulsed from Cemetery Ridge at Gettysburg, they left behind them at least thirty colors.

The tactical manuals of the day provided that the colors be "on the left of the right-centre company." This put the flag at the center of a regiment's first line, where it was certain to attract heavy fire. Destructive volleys against a regiment's color guard could affect the unit's cohesion, disrupting what in the twentieth century would be called the "command and control" of the regiment. More important to nineteenth-century soldiers, the flag was a trophy. Capturing an enemy's banner was undeniable evidence of a success in battle.

The tactical manuals called for a sergeant to serve as color-bearer — a soldier chosen by his colonel for his marching ability and "a just carriage of the person." This sergeant had a color guard of several corporals posted around him, but in the trauma of battle, any officer or man bold enough might pick up the flag if the color sergeant went down. The colonel of the Sixteenth Tennessee reported after Murfreesboro: "My flag-bearer (Sergeant Marberry) was disabled early in the charge. The flag was afterwards borne by Private Womack, who was also wounded. The flag-staff was broken and hit with balls in three places; the flag literally shot to pieces." When John Sedgwick's division was shot apart in the West Woods at Antietam, the color sergeant of the Thirty-fourth New York was wounded five times before dropping his flag. Nine days after Gettysburg, an officer of the Fourth Michigan described his regiment's defense of its flag in the Wheatfield: "A rebel officer had seized the colors of the 4th," Lt. Charles Salter wrote, "and Col. Jeffreys was defending it with his sword, when he was bayonetted by the rebels, as also the color bearer, and many others, who were trying to recover the colors."

While color-bearers attracted inordinate attention from the enemy, the truth was that every man who went forward with an assaulting line was in deadly peril. In 1864 William B. Hazen identified the main cause of this danger: the "accurate shooting rifle" had "replaced the random firing musket." The accuracy and range of rifle shoulder arms allowed defenders to deliver deadly volleys across hundreds of yards. Defending troops learned to increase this advantage with field entrenchments, which appeared more often and became more sophisticated as the war went on. Most Civil War battlefields were dominated by defending fire from well-protected infantrymen armed with rifles and artillerymen with smoothbore cannons. The chaplain of the First Massachusetts, who witnessed several charges during the May 1864 Battle of the Wilderness, saw that the defense consistently had the upper hand. "Whenever the Federal troops moved forward," he observed, "the Rebels appeared to have the advantage. Whenever they advanced, the advantage was transferred to us."

Assaulting troops often suffered horrifying losses. The Twentieth Massachusetts was one of many Union regiments that were broken apart in the senseless charges against Marye's Heights at Fredericksburg. The Twentieth advanced stubbornly and volleyed with the Confederates when the other regiments in its brigade fell back. It suffered over 160 killed and wounded, more than two-thirds of its number. While the second day's battle at Gettysburg hung in the balance, Maj. Gen. Winfield Scott Hancock called on the First Minnesota for a desperate assault. The regiment responded with an unsupported charge that cost the unit 82 percent of its effectives and left a captain in command of the regiment. During the bloodbath attacks at Cold Harbor on June 3, 1864, the Twenty-fifth Massachusetts suffered total casualties of 70 percent. The regiment had nearly reached the Confederate entrenchments, when, its colonel reported, it was "met by a storm of bullets, shot and shell that no human power could withstand." The survivors took what cover they could find and dug rifle pits with their hands and tin cups.

Confederate units also suffered enormous casualties on the offensive — staggering losses that the South, with fewer soldiers than the North, could not afford. In one of the war's fiercest counterassaults, Gen. John Bell Hood led his division into the Miller cornfield at Sharpsburg. The Fourth Texas, whose men were described by their lieutenant colonel as "half clad, many of them barefoot, and . . . only half fed for days before," lost more than 50 percent of its number in this action. The First Texas advanced on the left of the Fourth, carried 226 men and officers into the cornfield, and lost at least 182, roughly 80 percent of the regiment. Brig. Gen. George E. Pickett's charge at Gettysburg cost the South total casualties of over 6,400, about 62 percent of the soldiers who made the advance. Contemporary and postwar studies of several regiments put their total losses at more than 80 percent, and a few companies claimed losses of over 90 percent. Company A of the Eleventh North Carolina, in James J. Pettigrew's division, had entered the campaign with 100 men and officers. After the great assault on July 3, it was reduced to 8 men and a lone officer. The color company of the Thirty-eighth North Carolina was annihilated. Of the 32 field officers in Pickett's division, only 1 returned to Seminary Ridge unhurt. On November 30, 1864, the Army of Tennessee suffered over 5,500 casualties in its assault at Franklin. A union staff officer recalled that the Confederates "threw themselves against the works, fighting with what seemed the very madness of despair." Six Southern generals were killed or mortally wounded, 5 were wounded but survived, and 1 was captured. More than 50 regimental commanders became casualties.

The fate of Maj. Gen. Patrick R. Cleburne's division at Franklin epitomized the heroic tragedy of many Civil War attacks. The division made a long advance, longer than Pickett's at Gettysburg, across open fields. General Cleburne lost two horses and then went forward on foot until he was killed in front of the Union entrenchments. His command was shattered by artillery and rifle fire, leaving hundreds of Southern dead and wounded strewn along the Columbia Pike and near the Federal works. In Brig. Gen. Hiram B. Granbury's brigade, the commander was shot in the face and killed, his chief of staff was killed, and three regimental commanders were reported missing. Ten days after the battle, Granbury's brigade, and all its regiments, were commanded by captains. "The wonder is," one Union infantryman reflected, "that any of them escaped death or capture."

"Ducit Amor Patriae" reads the rather ungrammatical Latin phrase over the door. Its intent is clear. Imploring that they be led onward for the love of their native land, these citizen-soldiers, many of them still in mufti, present a scene repeated in thousands of small towns North and South as the young manhood of America stepped forward to enlist by the millions. (USAMHI)

Recruiting stations like this one on Hilton Head, South Carolina, photographed on September 8, 1864, urged the two nations to send forth their sons to fill the newborn regiments. (USAMHI)

Once enlisted, the recruits saw their first taste of the military life in training camps like this one: Camp Butler, near Springfield, Illinois. Over and over again, they worked at their evolutions until they got them right—or as near right as American volunteers ever became proficient at drill. (USAMHI)

Once trained, their weapons at hand, the novice soldiers posed proudly before the cameras. Their uniforms new, their arms brightly polished, they were as innocent as the nations sending them to war. Men of the Twelfth New York in a Mathew Brady & Company image made in 1861. (USAMHI)

The Twenty-second New York State Militia, men of Company D, pose at Harpers Ferry, Virginia, well equipped, and with some touches of home about "The Rendezvous." (USAMHI)

The Confederates, too, had homey tents for the new recruits. The Clinch Rifles, men of the Fifth Georgia, proudly display the Stars and Bars, their new national flag, from their tent pole. Within only a few months after the outbreak of war, such a well-supplied Confederate tent will be a rarity. The bright weapons, the new uniforms and full knapsacks, even the tent itself, will seem like luxuries in the days ahead. Only the black servant is likely to remain a constant. (USAMHI)

Bottom left: The Oglethorpe Infantry, Company D of the First Georgia, show what a new Rebel regiment looked like drawn up in formation for the camera. (USAMHI)

Bottom right: Formations played a big role in the new regiments' training. An unidentified company of Yankees goes through part of their daily drill for the camera. . . . (USAMHI)

. . . And this time, the company poses with their musicians drawn up to provide the march step. (USAMHI)

The regiments spent their days in camps like this one near Alexandria, Virginia. Maj. A. J. Russell, the North's only official army photographer, made this image of the camp of the Eleventh United States Infantry on April 3, 1864. (USAMHI)

Tented camps in summer and log-hut winter camps sprang up all across the continent. Here, in Grove Camp, the Twenty-fifth Massachusetts passes a winter near New Bern, North Carolina. (USAMHI)

There were a few pastimes available to the soldiers of North and South: reading, letter writing, friendly games of cards and dominoes, and whatever else the boys could invent to fill their idle hours. Here, men of the Third New Hampshire's Company F divert themselves at Hilton Head in 1862. (USAMHI)

Just visiting with friends and messmates, like these men of the 153d Pennsylvania, got the soldier through another day. (USAMHI)

Even posing for the camera's eye was a novelty — so much so that very few images of the men in their camps have a truly "candid" look about them. A wooden pose was the order of the day. (USAMHI)

Posing grew to grander scales when regiments like the Thirtieth Pennsylvania embellished their winter camps with laurel archways. Here Company A stands proudly before their handiwork. (USAMHI)

And nearby, Company B does the same. (USAMHI)

Some regiments even displayed their battle credits, listing their defeats, like Fredericksburg, along with their victories. (USAMHI)

Of course, there were always bands to play. Here, the drum corps of the Ninety-third New York in August 1863. (USAMHI)

And here, the bandsmen of the Thirtieth Pennsylvania Reserves. In actual battle, when not drumming they were expected to act as litter-bearers, helping remove the wounded from the field. (USAMHI)

A more established and permanent installation could afford to maintain a more elaborate band. Fort Monroe, near Norfolk, Virginia, remained in Union hands throughout the war, and its beplumed bandsmen sported all manner of instruments. (USAMHI)

Of more immediate and more lasting interest to the soldiers in the Yank and Reb regiments was food — rarely appetizing, and often scarce. A good cook could be a popular fellow. The cook's galley of H Company, Third New Hampshire, at Hilton Head shows "cookie" at work, with the implements of his trade nearby. (USAMHI)

What the commissary did not supply, the men could supplement for themselves from the sutlers, quasi-official vendors who followed the armies. Some sutlers erected substantial stores to peddle their books and pies and candles and whiskey, but most set up less elaborate affairs, like this one — a simple tent with a bar inside. Very few were likely to boast a man like the fellow at right, unsteadily balancing a couple of buckets on his head. (USAMHI)

Top left: A bottle of wine was always popular with the boys, and these oenophiles had their own "cellar" beneath a floorboard. (USAMHI)

Top right: The fortunate, usually officers, might even entertain members of their family in quieter times. Men of the 125th Ohio here lounge for the camera with wives and sons. (USAMHI)

The camera was ever popular. The private soldier loved to stand for it in the studio, posing in full uniform, weapon at the ready. (USAMHI)

They slicked back their hair, polished their buckles and buttons, and held fondly to their swords and sashes, like Sgt. R. W. Bowles here. (USAMHI)

And groups of comrades like these five unidentified Yankees formed a seemingly endless procession into the tent studios to sit for group portraits to send back home or to keep as mementos of the most important events of their lives. (USAMHI)

While on the march, their homes were quickly and simply erected and taken down again. But when the cold weather came, more permanent winter camps arose, like this virtual town of log-and-canvas houses built by the Fiftieth New York Engineers near Rappahannock Station, Virginia, in the winter of 1863/64. (USAMHI)

Whole forests could be denuded as the log houses — and, apparently, a log-and-mud smokehouse shaped like a teepee — were built. Here the structure serves as backdrop for members of the 164th and 170th New York. (USAMHI)

The round Sibley tents set atop wooden palisades in the camp of the 153d New York each boasted a tree or two outside its door. The soldiers tried to take something of home with them wherever they went. (USAMHI)

The Confederates, too, built winter quarters — though, as usual, they had to make do with less. Men believed to be from the First Texas built this log hut at Camp Quantico, near Dumfries, Virginia, in the winter of 1861/62. They named their "Beauregard Mess" for one of their Southern heroes, Gen. P. G. T. Beauregard, the man who took Fort Sumter. (RM)

Regiments doing more permanent garrison duty could luxuriate in much more lasting—and comfortable—quarters, like these barracks at Sandy Hook, New Jersey. (USAMHI)

Bottom left: And on Bedloe's Island, in New York Harbor, the barracks were positively lush. (USAMHI)

Bottom right: Wherever they were, the regiments built more than their own quarters. They took their God with them, and built modest chapels for worship. Here, the church of the Fourth Massachusetts Cavalry. (USAMHI)

Leave it to engineers, of course, to go a bit further, as some New Yorkers did with this regimental church at Poplar Grove, Virginia, in 1864. (USAMHI)

Top: When the men were ill, there were field hospitals for them, like this modest infirmary for the Third New Hampshire on Hilton Head. (USAMHI)

Bottom: When they misbehaved, there was always the provost marshal to police them and their camps. This is the provost's headquarters in the Army of the James at Bermuda Hundred, Virginia, in the winter of 1864/65. (USAMHI)

Conditions were much the same for the regiments whether they served east or west of the Alleghenies, though the westerners had a rawboned, more rugged look to them. These men of the 125th Ohio's Company C show the somewhat rumpled yet determined character of the men who did their fighting between the mountains and the Mississippi. (USAMHI)

Yet they, too, had their bands. Here, the "Tiger Band" of the 125th Ohio. (USAMHI)

And they, too, liked to pose for the camera. Officers of an unidentified western regiment sit and stand stiffly in their full uniforms, and then, for the fun of it, . . . (USAMHI)

. . . they sit again in their shirt sleeves as the troops huddle round. (USAMHI)

The variety of the uniforms that they wore, East and West, North and South, was dazzling. It is a shame that the cameras of the day could not capture in all their gaudy color a regiment of zouaves like the 164th New York at guard mounting . . . (USAMHI)

. . . or the 114th Pennsylvania, with its turbans, shown here at Petersburg, Virginia, in August 1864. (USAMHI)

Even the 114th's band wore the outfit, which looked more like a fraternal lodge's regalia than soldier's dress. (USAMHI)

The Confederates had their fancy zouave units as well. Though they do not show well in this damaged old print by New Orleans photographer J. D. Edwards, Coppen's Louisiana Zouaves wore the colorful baggy pants and fezzes borrowed from the French army pattern. (SHC)

And here another New Orleans photographer has caught yet another Louisiana zouave unit standing at ease in 1861. (LC)

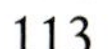

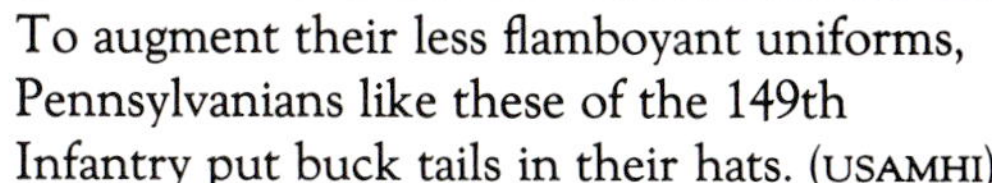

To augment their less flamboyant uniforms, Pennsylvanians like these of the 149th Infantry put buck tails in their hats. (USAMHI)

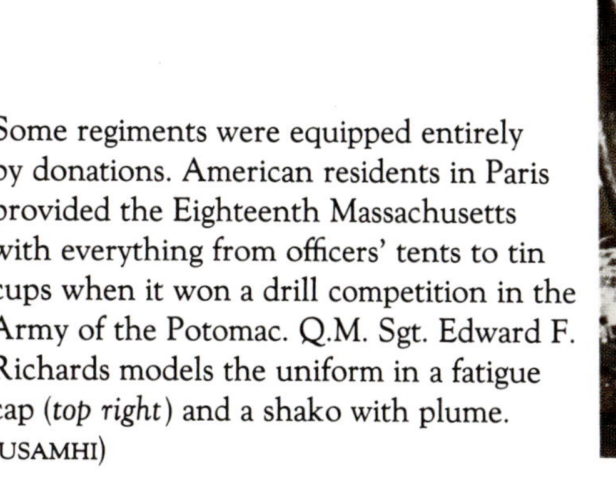

Some regiments were equipped entirely by donations. American residents in Paris provided the Eighteenth Massachusetts with everything from officers' tents to tin cups when it won a drill competition in the Army of the Potomac. Q.M. Sgt. Edward F. Richards models the uniform in a fatigue cap (*top right*) and a shako with plume. (USAMHI)

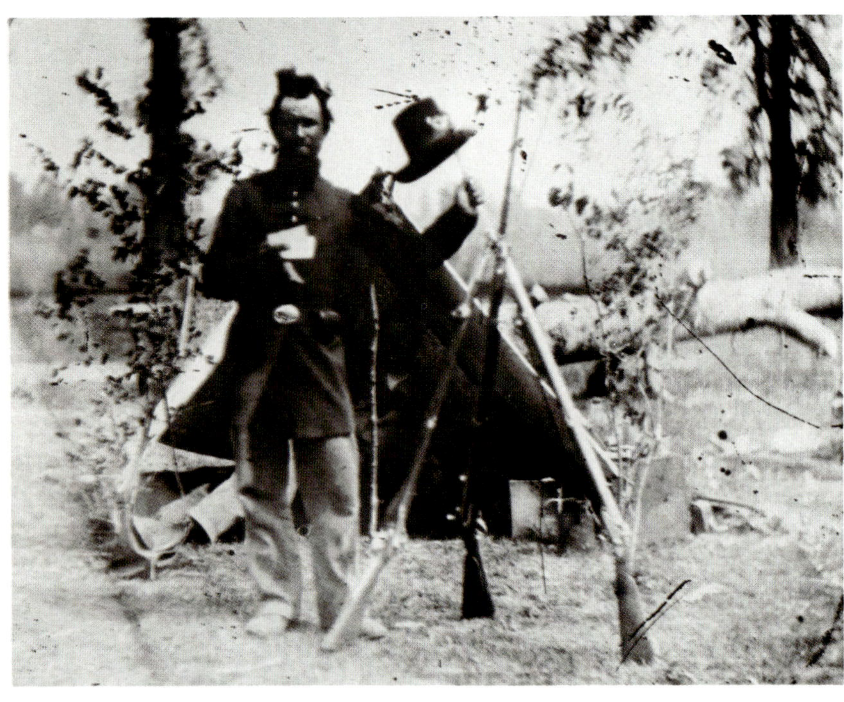

Even among the more commonly equipped regiments, there was still considerable variety. Some, for instance, wore nothing more distinctive from the average than the Hardee hat — though usually on their heads and not their bayonets. (RM)

The so-called regular regiments — like the Eighth United States Infantry, shown here at Fairfax Court House, Virginia, in June 1863 — wore uniformly standard clothing with almost nothing to set them apart from the volunteer outfits. (USAMHI)

Some regiments adopted mascots, though none became more famous than Old Abe, the eagle that accompanied the Eighth Wisconsin through the war. Here he perches atop a Union shield as men of the regiment's color guard pose near Vicksburg, Mississippi. (OCHM)

Particularly in the Confederacy, militia and home guard units that existed before the war enlisted en masse and wore their old uniforms into the new service. Men of the Kentucky State Guard pose here at their 1860 encampment at Louisville. A year later, wearing the same dress, most of them would go into the various regiments that formed the Bluegrass State's famous Confederate Orphan Brigade. (KHS)

Whatever their background and nativity, the men in the ranks formed thousands of regiments North and South, and theirs was the task of fighting the war. The 139th Pennsylvania stands ready for the fray. (USAMHI)

They stood at attention all across the war-torn continent — like Company A of the First Connecticut Heavy Artillery, shown here in 1863. (USAMHI)

Top left: When not in battle, they could lounge like these men of the De Kalb regiment's Company C, in the old Confederate fortifications at Manassas, Virginia. (USAMHI)

Top right: They might stand doing garrison duty in exotic places like Hilton Head, South Carolina, where Company H of the Third New Hampshire looks martial indeed for the camera of H. P. Moore. (USAMHI)

Bottom right: Or they might sprawl about at their training camps, like this one in Readville, Massachusetts, where the Forty-fifth Massachusetts sits ready to march off to war. (USAMHI)

The cavalry were ready, too — horsemen like these, of the First Massachusetts's Company G, shown at Edisto Island, South Carolina, in 1862. Already bloodied in battle, they would do their part in this war. (USAMHI)

And so would the men who manned the big guns — men like those of Pennsylvania's famed Keystone Battery, with their cannons, caissons, and limbers ready for action. (USAMHI)

All across the continent they were marching. (USAMHI)

The fields of America were filled with soldiers practicing and drilling. The Second Rhode Island near Washington in the winter of 1861/62. (USAMHI)

They stood at dress parade, like these men of the First Rhode Island Cavalry near Manassas in July 1862. (USAMHI)

They stood rank upon rank in their masonry fastnesses, such as Fort Pulaski, Georgia, here held by the Forty-eighth New York. (USAMHI)

And they fought and bled in a thousand little, unknown places, like these men of the Second New York Heavy Artillery posing at Fort C. F. Smith, near Washington. (USAMHI)

Sometimes they took horrible losses. The First Minnesota, whose officers are shown here at Fort Snelling in 1861 before the regiment went to the front, was almost destroyed in the war. (MHS)

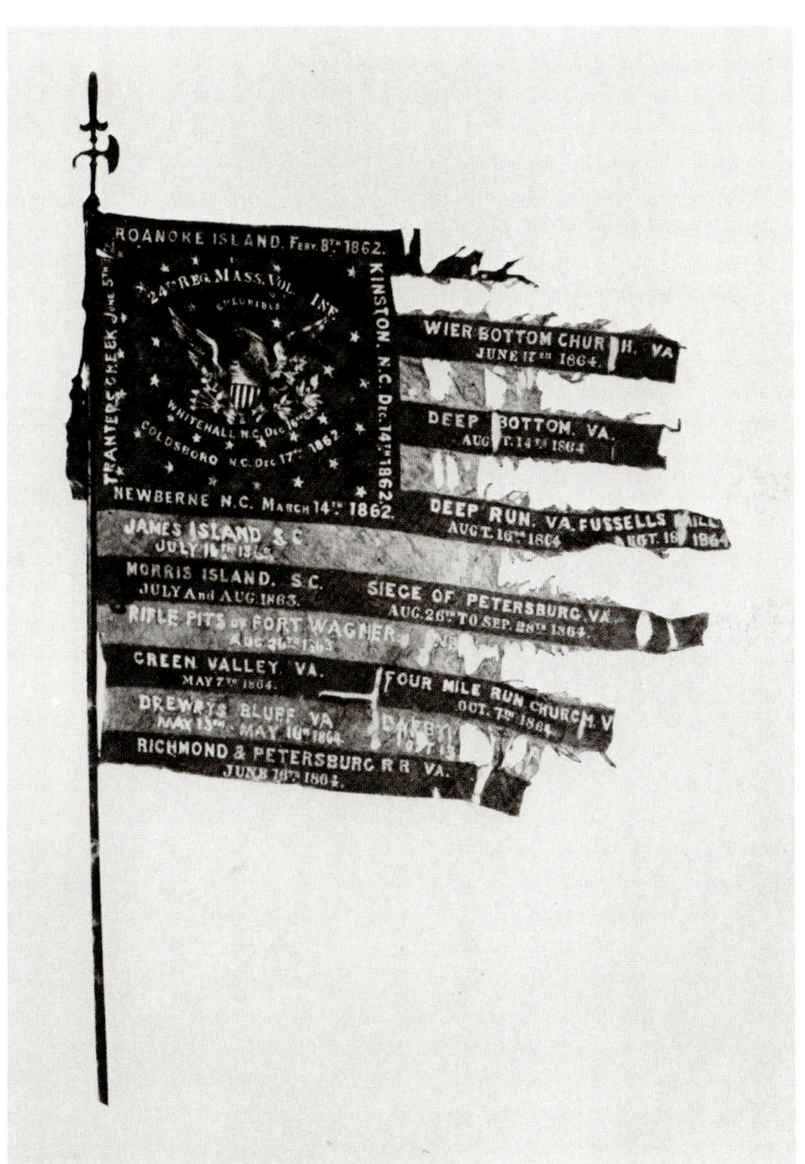

The story showed in their flags, the bits of fabric for which the men fought and died. The colors of the Twenty-fourth Massachusetts displayed the unit's battle credits, and showed the wear of the camp and the field. (USAMHI)

Those of the Nineteenth Massachusetts were reduced to hanging tatters by the rigors of battle. (USAMHI)

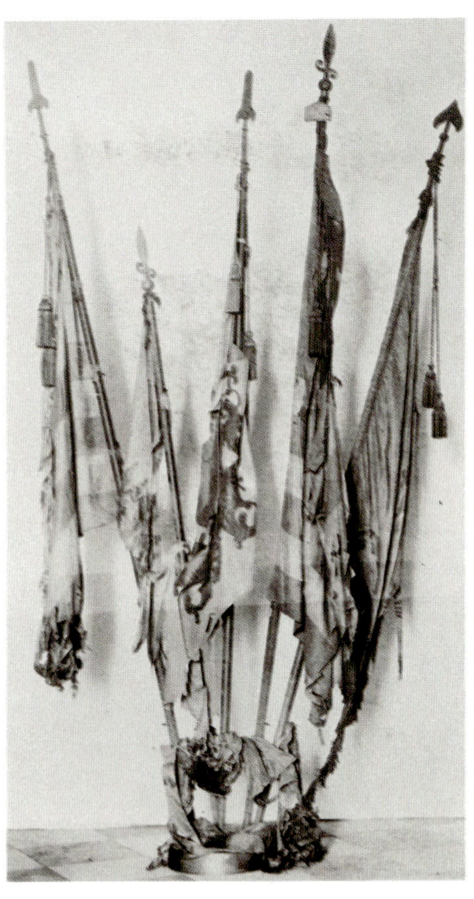

And here, the colors of the Fortieth Massachusetts are barely a memory of the once bright flags that went off to war. (USAMHI)

The banners, like the regiments who marched under them during America's greatest trial, have receded into dim memories only fleetingly recalled from the fading images of the past. During the Seven Days Battles near Richmond in the summer of 1862, some unknown Yankee dropped this tintype of his company on the battleground, where another Yank found it. This disappearing photograph is what we have left to remind us of them—and of the deeds of the men in the ranks. (USAMHI)

Of Ships and Seamen

Adm. Ernest M. Eller

SEAPOWER, which has helped shape America's destiny in every generation, played a role of first importance in the Civil War. The United States is a giant "island" nation. Blessed with vast resources, a benign climate, a free people, and open access to the oceans, she early seemed destined for world leadership. Had the war ended differently, this destiny might not have reached fruition. It *would* have ended differently except for the North's maritime superiority.

Although Lincoln, Lee, Grant, and others did at the time, too few since have comprehended the giant hand of the sea in this struggle between brothers. Had the North prosecuted the war afloat with less energy, or the South more effectively, the history of the nation could have been significantly changed.

The North laid the keel for certain victory in the first two years of the war, and that victory hinged on maritime superiority. The meaning of control of the water has seldom been more vividly brought home to American leaders than in the panic that engulfed them in March 1862. After the fall of the Norfolk Navy Yard in Virginia, the Confederates raised the USS *Merrimack* and converted the burned steam frigate into the CSS *Virginia,* a crude ironclad. On March 8, 1862, she steamed into Hampton Roads to sink the USS *Congress* and the USS *Cumberland.* Telegraph keys clicked madly. Consternation swept northward. At President Lincoln's emergency cabinet meeting desperation reigned. Some, striding about, kept looking out to see if the *Virginia* was coming up the Potomac!

In the unseen ways of Providence, during the night the USS *Monitor* — hastily built in five months, and nearly sunk by foul weather en route — eased into Hampton Roads. Even as the cabinet fearfully debated, she and the *Virginia* met in a dramatic duel of iron against iron. It was a draw, but this first battle of ironclads reverberated around the world. In the North, men relaxed from panic. In the South, high dreams collapsed. Overseas, England and France had begun ironclad navies, and their worth was improved. Now nations were shocked into the future.

Lincoln had proclaimed a blockade of Southern ports on April 19, 1861 — then largely a paper blockade. Only forty-two warships were in commission, and many of these cruised far-off seas. The South, however, had no navy, and could never acquire an important one, whereas the North had a large merchant marine with trained seamen, along with ample facilities to build and convert. Strong warships provided the nucleus for the blockade. They were rapidly augmented by minor ones, mostly converted steamers, ferries, and tugs. By year's end, active warships had nearly tripled. By Appomattox, they had increased by over thirtyfold.

While a blockade can reduce a port's commerce, only capture can surely stop it. The North's first notable victories came from supremacy at sea, in amphibious assaults. Blockade-runners and Confederate privateers used Hatteras Inlet, not far from Hampton Roads. Two weak sand forts, lightly garrisoned, guarded it. In August, enough ships having become available, an amphibious Federal force under Flag Off. Silas Stringham and Gen. Ben Butler attacked. The warships' heavy guns outclassed and outranged those ashore and easily blasted the forts into submission for Butler's troops to occupy.

The next target was Port Royal, a magnificent sound about halfway between heavily defended Charleston and Savannah. In November Flag Off. Samuel Du Pont skillfully maneuvered the largest fleet the nation had ever assembled in and out past Port Royal's entrance forts. In five hours of heavy pounding of the defenders from the rear and sea flanks, he forced evacuation of the forts. The sound soon became an important advance base for resupply of the blockading fleet, much increasing effective time on station. Now the blockade strangled tighter and tighter. Increasingly, raids from the sea ravaged the coast and up the rivers, wasting Confederate resources, draining manpower from main armies, eroding strength. Attack from the sea is hard to counter because of the inherent concentration of strength at the point of decision, swiftness of assault, and ease of surprise.

Had the war come a generation earlier, the outcome may have been different. Navies now had awesome capabilities. Through the centuries warships had gained increasing effectiveness in operations against the land. By 1861 the accelerating Industrial Revolution had brought quantum leaps — as in steam and iron, more powerful and accurate guns, protective armor. No longer were ships restricted by wind and tide. Now, with engines, they could come and go at will, even upstream in swift rivers. The increased speed, precision, and flexibility that steam gave to attack from afloat time after time proved decisive in combined or purely naval operations. Armored in iron, naval vessels became terrifying movable forts that could steam in close to advantageous positions. Rapidly firing their huge guns, they could overpower all but the heaviest fixed guns ashore.

The change to steam had been especially rapid on rivers. Industrial growth also increased the availability of iron for armor and stronger guns. These advances early forged Northern success on the western rivers. Comdr. John Rodgers, a hard-bitten old sea dog, went west in May 1861 to start an inland navy. Driving hard, he converted three river steamers and had them ready for service under the army with naval and pickup crews by early August. Immediately, in independent and combined operations, they began to demonstrate the immense benefit of strength afloat. Meanwhile, he contracted construction of semi-ironclad gunboats that would dominate the upper rivers.

On the same day that Port Royal fell, an amphibious operation down the Mississippi under little-known Brig. Gen. Ulysses Grant struck at Belmont, Missouri, to break up a concentration of Confederates threatening Federals advancing in this pro-Southern area. Striking swiftly by water, he surprised and routed the Confederates. Then, as his troops plundered their camp, Confederate reinforcements surprised and routed them. Grant's men fled to the transports as well-directed grape and canister from the wooden gunboats helped check the pursuers. Grant himself galloped to the bank and rode aboard just as the last boat cut its lines and pulled clear.

Debouching into the Ohio only twenty miles apart, the Tennessee and the Cumberland rivers open highways across Tennessee. Each had a guardian fort some miles upstream, and there the effect of inland seapower became dramatically evident in February 1862. The first armored gunboats having become available, a joint operation sailed up the Ohio to attack Fort Henry on the Tennessee, which was poorly sited on low ground. Landing the troops some miles below the fort, Flag Off. Andrew Foote, another rugged old salt, steamed to the very muzzles of the fort's cannons. On the swollen river his great guns loomed down on the defenders. In a fierce duel at point-blank range, the guns afloat knocked out those ashore, forcing surrender before the troops could arrive. The wooden gunboats now raced upriver across Tennessee to Muscle Shoals, Alabama, capturing ships (including a prospective ironclad), destroying supplies, spreading terror — an omen of the future.

Fort Donelson on the Cumberland, better situated on high ground, came next. Plunging fire from this much stronger position repelled the first attack of the tinclads, as the lightly armored gunboats were called, but they returned to rain death into the fort while Grant's troops overcame the defenders.

Fatefully, the Confederates had lost the water highways. No barrier now stood between the invaders and Nashville, a principal arsenal and industrial city many difficult miles away by land, but a different matter for steamboats. As Foote's gunboats raced upriver for the kill, the Confederates hastily quit gun batteries and abandoned Nashville with its needed factories and mountains of supplies.

Heavy guns on the water, spearhead for the army, made it possible to win in days of little cost what could not have been won in months of hard fighting, if at all, without them. A Nashville newspaper ruefully and forebodingly observed, "We had nothing to fear from a land attack but the gunboats are the devil."

The Confederate lines that extended far up into Kentucky had been breached. Now Federal troops poured through like a torrent. Supported and supplied along the water highways, Grant pressed south following the Tennessee River. On April 6 and 7, in the Battle of Shiloh — two shattering months for the South since Fort Henry — the Confederates surprised the invaders near Pittsburg Landing and drove them back to the river. "We were within . . . 150 to 400 yards of the enemy's position," reported Maj. Gen. Leonidas Polk, "and nothing seemed wanting to complete the most brilliant victory" over the demoralized Federals. Then wooden gunboats hurried to the point of decision "and opened a tremendous cannonade of shot and shell" into the Confederates. This hail of projectiles broke up the attack and swung the delicate balance of battle to the Union.

Meanwhile, the river ironclads, augmented by mortar boats, spearheaded an advance down the Mississippi. One after the other, "impregnable" positions fell to the mighty cannons and troop envelopment facilitated by control of the water. The record echoes like the clank of doom's chain rumbling out: Columbus, Kentucky, "Gibralter of the West," in March; strongly armed Island No. 10, "Key to the Mississippi," in April; Fort Pillow, last bastion before Memphis, in June. Now defenseless, this important commercial and industrial city surrendered to the gunboats on June 6, with troops soon following to occupy.

The Federal advance did not go uncontested, despite the fearsome tinclads. In addition to fortified positions that held out until outflanked, the Confederates vigorously developed from limited resources what naval strength they could. In 1861 they began to arm river craft as makeshift gunboats, then rams; they also began strong ironclads, but failed to give them high priority early enough. Although far outclassed, the little Southern warships gave battle. On one occasion, dashing out from Fort Pillow's protection, rams defeated two Union ironclads, sinking one. In a final gallant but doomed battle to save Memphis, the squadron sacrificed itself. With fort and warships gone, Memphis fell, and the Federal fleet ran on downstream to Vicksburg.

While combined operations rocked the Confederates on the upper rivers, a typhoon that would strike a mortal blow gathered to the south. Adm. David Farragut impatiently waited with some of the Union's most powerful warships while Comdr. David Porter's twenty mortar boats hurled huge projectiles day and night into the forts guarding New Orleans. Thousands of shells rained in. The mortar ammunition was nearly gone. The forts grimly held on. Would they prove impassable barriers?

Daring the "impossible" of forcing upstream past strong forts with wooden ships, Farragut lined his vessels' sides with heavy chain, rope, and hammocks. Then, during the midwatch darkness that opened April 24—a day of doom for the South—in a melee of shot and bursting shells, of fire rafts and death, the fleet drove past the guardians of New Orleans, and in the battle destroyed the small Confederate squadron that valiantly engaged. Steaming on upstream, the fleet reached the center of the South's largest city—its wealthiest, and a major shipping and export center. The flotilla's big guns, which the defenders could not match, loomed over the city, demanding surrender. One of the mighty unfinished ironclads that could possibly have saved the city, given a few more days to complete construction, floated by burning in a stream of blazing cotton bales and river craft—an image of the destiny of the South. Fewer than three thousand Yankee seamen had dealt a blow from which the Confederacy could never recover. Farragut appropriately called all hands to quarters to "return thanks to Almighty God for His great goodness and mercy."

Confederate captain John Maffitt later lamented: "The grand mistake of the South was neglecting her Navy. All our Army movements out West were baffled by the armed Federal steamers. . . . Before the capture of New Orleans the South ought to have had a Navy strong enough to prevent its capture. . . . Neglect of the Navy proved irremediable and fatal."

The government did try, but too late. The political leaders guessed wrong by initially embargoing export of cotton, instead of shipping freely and concentrating on obtaining warships. They failed to perceive until too late the awesome influence upon land operations of loss of the water.

The catastrophe of New Orleans cut off most of the South's cotton exports. Occupying this thriving port, and with the ultimate capture of Vicksburg, the Federals had sundered the South and opened the way to the sea for the North's vast and rich heartland.

The Vicksburg campaign was long and bitter. Farragut soon ran past the fortifications to join the river fleet. But over a year of joint operations and give-and-take conflict—including the short, brilliant career of the ironclad CSS *Arkansas*, which inflicted considerable damage on the Federal fleet—went by before the stronghold fell. Cut off by water and land, starving and with resources exhausted, the stouthearted defenders finally capitulated on July 4, 1863.

This campaign, with warships and troops working closely together, ended the first phase of naval support in combined operations. Through the remaining years, the role of strength afloat remained crucial. There were continual operations with troops along the streams—combined operations large and small, spreading destruction wherever gunboats would float. Often even a few big naval guns played a critical role. Unceasingly, warships interdicted Confederate troop movements, knocked out gun positions, assured the flow along the river highways of the armies' huge logistic needs. Day and night, they pressed the blockade along the coast and waterways, tightening the death noose.

In the East as in the West, Confederate concentrations and defenses were seldom safe within range of warships. Almost daily, attack from the water destroyed resources and installations, frustrated plans, disrupted or influenced troop movements. Even major Confederate campaigns had to consider pressure from the water. In his brilliant offensives, Lee was limited to inland sweeps clear of navigable waters. In his resolute defense of Richmond, he ever had the one-sided handicap of Federal control of the waterways.

The blockade tightened. Following Port Royal, other harbors fell or were ravaged. As Lee had perceived early in the war, "wherever [the enemy's] fleet can be brought," except at powerful fixed positions, "we have nothing to oppose its heavy guns, which sweep over the low banks of this country with irresistible force." By 1864 the South's only important exits to the sea—and these were heavily blockaded—were Mobile, Savannah, Charleston, and Wilmington. In August of that year, with a squadron that included new monitors, Farragut burst past the entrance forts, through minefields, into Mobile Bay. He lost the monitor *Tecumseh*, but captured the ironclad CSS *Tennessee* and closed the bay.

Against the ever-growing Federal navy, the Confederates had even less chance in these last years. Yet at every opportunity, ingeniously and valiantly, they struck hard. On January 1, 1863, improvised "cottonclads" dashed out of Galveston to rout the small blockading squadron. Later that month, the ironclad rams *Chicora* and *Palmetto State* steamed from Charleston in a fog to shatter blockaders. Protected by iron or cotton, rams were especially effective in several minor engagements.

The Confederacy began building some fifty ironclads of sorts, but, hampered by limited resources, scant facilities, government priorities, and vigorous Federal advances, as at New Orleans, got only a few into effective action. Their chief value to the South was in the delay completed ones imposed on Union movements, and in their large roles in helping to save Savannah, Charleston, and Richmond down to the closing days of the war.

Moored mines called "torpedoes" were extensively used, and claimed their first victim in sinking the USS *Cairo* during the Vicksburg campaign; their greatest success came in sinking the powerful *Tecumseh*, eliciting Farragut's historic shout, "Damn the torpedoes!" Despite imperfect firing devices, these lurking menaces destroyed two score Union vessels by Appomattox — dark omen of the future and today's deadly sophisticated mines. Had the South pushed their production early on, they could have had large impact.

Boats mounting spar torpedoes had some effect, notably in damaging the ironclad USS *New Ironsides* off Charleston. The submersible *H. L. Hunley*, a converted boiler propelled by men turning cranks, on a dark night steered into the Charleston blockading squadron and rammed a torpedo into the USS *Housatonic*. The victim sank, but so did the *Hunley*. For the third time, dedicated men perished in her; but this notable first sinking by a submarine cast long shadows ahead to the increasingly more potent undersea monsters of our time.

The chief material injury to the North at sea came from commerce raiders, especially the *Alabama*, the *Florida*, and the *Shenandoah*. Her crew unaware of the end of the war, the latter continued to destroy whalers in the Bering Sea through July 1865. The Confederate cruisers dealt damage that the American merchant marine would not recover from for generations. Besides vessels lost, Yankee shipowners transferred hundreds to foreign registry. Yet this economic loss had little effect on the final outcome. With control of the oceans, the Union could still draw on the resources of the world, whereas the South, with far greater need, got only crumbs past the blockade in these last years.

The ceaseless and overwhelming benefits of power afloat continued inexorably for the North through 1864 and into early 1865 as hope ended for the strangled, sundered, and battered South. With the navy controlling the rivers, Grant maneuvered south of Richmond. Setting up a tremendous headquarters — supply base at City Point, protected by the navy — and with logistic needs pouring in by ship, his army settled in for victory.

Cutting loose from river and railroad supply routes, Sherman took Atlanta, then marched to the sure haven of sea support at Savannah. Thence he set his march north, close enough to the coast for ready support or retirement. The Confederates evacuated Charleston, which lacked landward defenses. After an initial setback, a massive amphibious attack force, shielded by the heavy fire of the largest fleet the United States would assemble until the twentieth century, took Fort Fisher. Lee's last gateway for necessities abroad slammed shut.

Desperately in want, Lee's weakening army struggled on with prospects shrinking daily. The Confederate ironclads on the James tried to attack Grant's base at City Point, but were frustrated. Success could have had momentous effect on the campaign. At last history's noblest and one of her ablest generals surrendered his tattered but undaunted faithfuls at Appomattox. Genius ashore, lacking indispensable power afloat, had succumbed to the combined, crushing force of might on land and sea.

None of man's ceaseless wars has brought out more heroism, fortitude, and sacrifice on both sides than was exhibited from Bull Run to Appomattox. Yet anyone studying all aspects of the war finds it difficult to escape the conclusion that the North's superiority afloat, against gallant resistance, helped swing the balance to victory.

One thing that both Union and Confederate navies had in common was the training ground of their officers, the U.S. Naval Academy at Annapolis. (USAMHI)

Another was that, thanks to their training there, officers of both sides revered the same naval heroes of old — men memorialized in monuments at the academy. (USAMHI)

And as midshipmen, they had all been young together once. During the war, the Union moved the academy to Newport, Rhode Island, where these young men gathered for the camera, but their faces might easily have been those of a score of classes before them. (NHC)

As everywhere else in the young nation, the war on the water began in a hesitant and makeshift fashion. The first U.S. officer killed in a water action was Comdr. James H. Ward, who was patrolling the Potomac in his little converted side-wheel steamer *Freeborn*. On June 27, 1861, off Mathias Point, he was sighting one of his three guns when an enemy bullet gave him a mortal wound. This 1861 image is a reenactment. The man kneeling behind the gun on the *Freeborn* is wearing Ward's hat and jacket, and posing just as Ward was when hit. The new war was still a novelty when men could restage its tragic events. (USAMHI)

Top right: Many of the Union's warships were makeshifts, including converted Staten Island ferryboats like this one, the *Commodore Morse,* whose fore and aft decks were lightly protected with iron bulwarks and ungainly mounted naval cannons. (USAMHI)

Bottom left: Some of these ferryboats would do good service for years, and their officers were justly proud. Despite their previous histories, these were warships now. (USAMHI)

Bottom right: With the need to transport large numbers of men and supplies, Uncle Sam turned to other commercial vessels, since the existing merchant fleet far outnumbered the naval ships available. Steamers like the *Sacramento* of the Pacific Mail Steam Ship Company soon found themselves pressed into service. (USAMHI)

It needed only a few deck guns, and any peaceful vessel like the *Arago* could find itself transformed into a warship. (USAMHI)

The Confederates, too, had to make do at first, either with what they could capture from the Federals or what they could convert. J. D. Edwards's camera caught this view in Pensacola, Florida, in early 1861, of the side-wheeler *Fulton*, which was just being refitted when the navy yard fell to the Rebels. Now, they hoped, the ship and all that ammunition in neat pyramids before it, would be used against the Yankees. (SHC)

The Union's first blow — and in the end, its most effective — was the blockade. Scores of warships like the USS *Marblehead* would do seemingly endless months of duty in patrolling Confederate harbors. (USAMHI)

Here Edwards's camera captured a Yankee ship — perhaps the flag of truce boat *Wyandotte* — lying at anchor off Fort Pickens, near Pensacola. Confederates would see this and a lot more enemy ships at their harbor mouths, slowly strangling the South. (SHC)

But only Edwards and one or two others would ever record the scene of the Yankee blockaders. Here, he caught the *Macedonian*, again in front of Fort Pickens. (USAMHI)

Every kind of vessel joined the blockade while the North feverishly rushed to build its fleet. Side-wheelers like the old USS *Mingo* . . . (USAMHI)

. . . joined more sleek vessels, like the *Boxer*, which itself had the look of a blockade-runner, . . . (USAMHI)

. . . and more workmanlike vessels, like the USS *Magnolia*, of the East Gulf Blockading Squadron. Wherever there was Southern coastline, the Yankees tried to stop commerce. (USAMHI)

Halting Confederate trade required substantial bases on the enemy coastline, in order to refit and supply the blockaders, and Hilton Head, South Carolina, became one of the first and best. Captured in 1862, it remained in Yankee hands thereafter, and the line of warships coming into it was as seemingly endless as the anchor chains laid out in the foreground here. (USAMHI)

It required a few alterations. Mr. Pope's house, with its fine ocean view, became . . . (USAMHI)

. . . a signal station, for communicating with the ships at sea. (USAMHI)

The scenes aboard the blockading ships themselves were much the same no matter the vessel. The gun deck of the USS *Pocahontas* is quite shipshape, from the polished guns and neatly coiled ropes, to the canvas wind vane (in front of the stack) used to catch breezes and divert them into the bowels of the ship. (USAMHI)

Mostly just the faces of the crewmen and the guns they served differed. Here a mortar schooner's big gun looms behind the mainmast. (USAMHI)

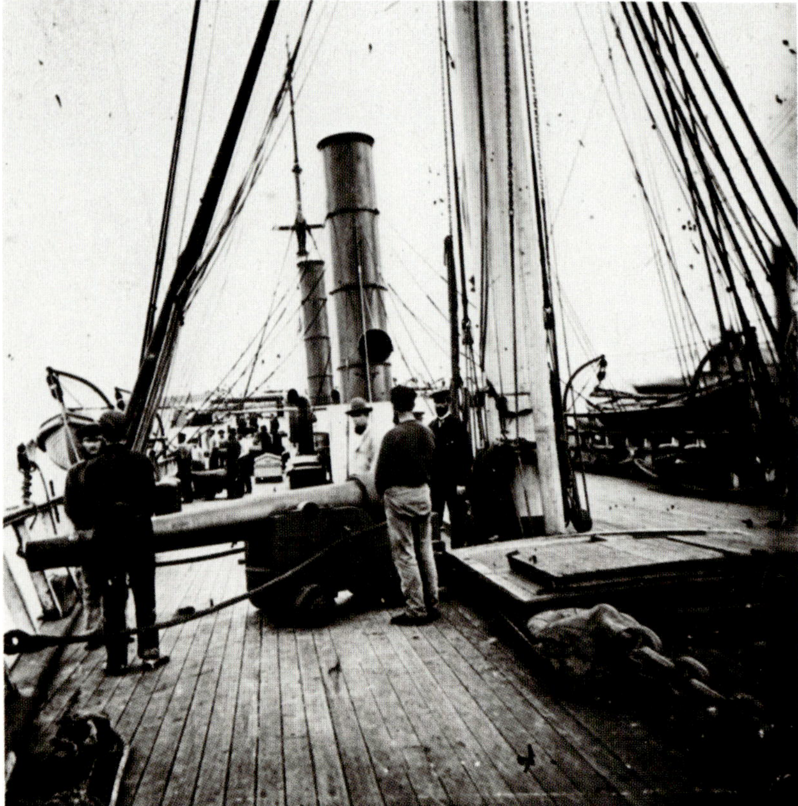

Top left: Looking forward there were guns. (USAMHI)

Top right: Looking aft there were guns. (USAMHI)

Bottom left: Seemingly on every deck in the hemisphere there were guns. (USAMHI)

All those ships required a lot of fuel, and the Union navy maintained huge coal wharves like this one at Alexandria, Virginia, to keep its ships steaming. (USAMHI)

Every river and inlet on the Confederate coastline had to be watched, and none more so than the James River, where transports supplied Grant's army in 1864 and naval vessels vied with enemy shore batteries. (USAMHI)

Wherever it went, Lincoln's navy built its own docks, as here at City Point, on the James. (USAMHI)

And the procession of steamers that plied the rivers, unloading at those docks and heading back north for more, was endless. (USAMHI)

Now and then, the warships of both sides contested the rivers, and when they did meet in battle, it could be epic. No fight in naval history is more famous than that between the CSS *Virginia*—of which no photograph survives—and the USS *Monitor*. The *Monitor*'s foredeck and turret appear here in this 1862 image, showing well some of the dents made by enemy shot during the battle. (USAMHI)

Another dreaded Confederate ironclad was the *Albemarle,* which severely damaged several Yankee ships in North Carolina's Roanoke River before intrepid raiders sank her. The ironclad appears here after being raised in 1865. (NHC)

More formidable still was the CSS *Atlanta.* She was deemed sufficiently powerful that after the Federals captured her in 1863, they put her in the Union service on the James. (USAMHI)

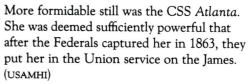

Sustaining all these warships required a massive transport fleet — unsung heroes of the war on the water. The steamer *Liberty* shown in September 1864. (USAMHI)

The transport *Westmorland*, photographed in June 1864. The forest of masts behind her gives evidence of the number of ships in port at any one time in the Union's harbors. (USAMHI)

Top left: The names of many vessels have been forgotten. (USAMHI)

Bottom left: As have the names behind the faces that sailed them in supplying the Union war effort. (USAMHI)

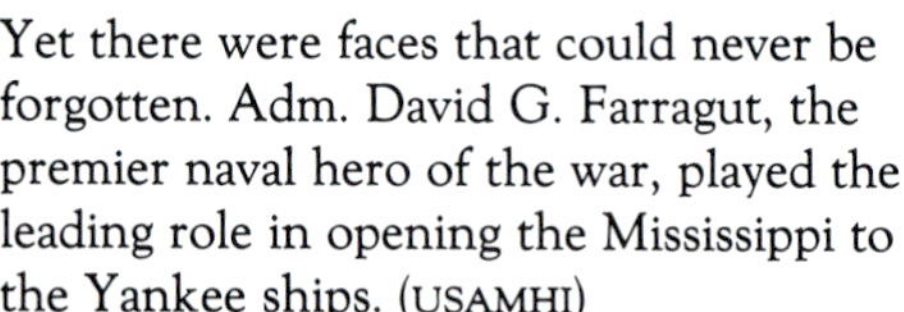

Yet there were faces that could never be forgotten. Adm. David G. Farragut, the premier naval hero of the war, played the leading role in opening the Mississippi to the Yankee ships. (USAMHI)

His famous ship *Hartford*, shown here at Boston around 1859, took him from victory to victory on the river and in the Gulf. (LC)

Other ships accompanied Farragut when he took New Orleans in April 1862. The USS *Portsmouth* (at left), lined with guns from stem to stern, was one of the most formidable. (USAMHI)

Bottom left: Old river "woodclads" like the *Conestoga,* shown here in an A. D. Lytle image, fought with Farragut in opening the Father of Waters. (USAMHI)

Bottom right: Another, damaged, Lytle image shows the USS *Albatross,* one of Farragut's warships, whose commander, John Hart, died apparently of suicide while on the river. In a spirit of brotherhood stronger than the hatred of war, the Freemason was buried ashore at Saint Francisville, Louisiana, by fellow Masons who were Confederates. (USAMHI)

Captured Confederate ships were turned to Yankee uses here on the Mississippi, too. The CSS *General Bragg* fell into Union hands and thereafter plied the Mississippi for its onetime enemies. (USAMHI)

Whole fleets of the city-class ironclads steamed on the western waters in support of land operations. Beyond the moored barges in the foreground, the *De Kalb* sits at left, with the *Cincinnati* in the center and the *Mound City* at right. (NYHS)

They were mighty behemoths. The *Louisville* here rests by the bank off Memphis. (USAMHI)

The *Baron De Kalb*, formerly the *Saint Louis*, was arguably the first ironclad of the war, having been launched October 12, 1861. With her thirteen guns, she was easily one of the most powerful. (USAMHI)

Yet there were even bigger river giants on the Mississippi. Lytle's camera caught the mammoth *Choctaw*, off Baton Rouge. (USAMHI)

One of Farragut's trusty subordinates on the river was his stepbrother, David D. Porter. (USAMHI)

From his flagship the *Black Hawk*, Porter assisted vitally in the taking of Vicksburg as well as in later campaigns on the western rivers. This image shows her off Memphis in June 1864, just a few months before an accidental fire destroyed the valiant ship. (USAMHI)

Top left: Scores of the little tinclads patrolled the waters of the Mississippi and its tributaries. Many of their names are unknown, as with this substantial-looking vessel caught by Lytle's lens. (USAMHI)

Top right: For other tinclads we have names and numbers. Lytle photographed the *Nymph*, No. 54, as she lay anchored off the Baton Rouge shore. (USAMHI)

There were even hospital ships, the first of their kind, to house and care for the naval wounded. The *Red Rover*, a captured Confederate vessel, was a familiar sight on the Mississippi. (USAMHI)

Up some of the broader tributaries, like the Tennessee River, smaller supply steamers kept up a constant pace as they shuttled war materiel to the troops fighting in the interior. A besieged army in Chattanooga was virtually saved by the supplies brought upriver by little ships like this one. (USAMHI)

Some of the little steamers bore the names of battles, like the *Chickamauga*, but more important than that, they carried tons of needed supplies. (USAMHI)

As quickly as possible those supplies were unloaded and, empty, the little vessels went back downriver for more. (USAMHI)

The transports came in for their share of fighting, too, when Confederate cavalry became fond of attacking them from the shoreline. In the campaign up Louisiana's Red River, the *Black Hawk* (a different ship entirely from Porter's flagship) was attacked by Rebel batteries on the banks. Some of the holes from enemy shot are still visible. (USAMHI)

Of course, there was a war of sorts on the oceans as well, though it was largely one of hunter and pursued. Mighty Union warships like this unidentified steamer cruised the waters of the world looking for the dreaded Confederate commerce raiders. . . . (CA)

. . . Their most sought-after quarry was this man, Capt. Raphael Semmes, and his ship the *Alabama*. Man and ship were both photographed here, probably off Cape Town, South Africa. Semmes's executive officer, John M. Kell, stands in the background. (IMP)

Almost as feared as the *Alabama* was the CSS *Florida*, the large vessel in the center of this image made at Madeira in 1864. Federal naval authorities used this photograph in the hope that it would help identify the ship when and if she were found. (NA)

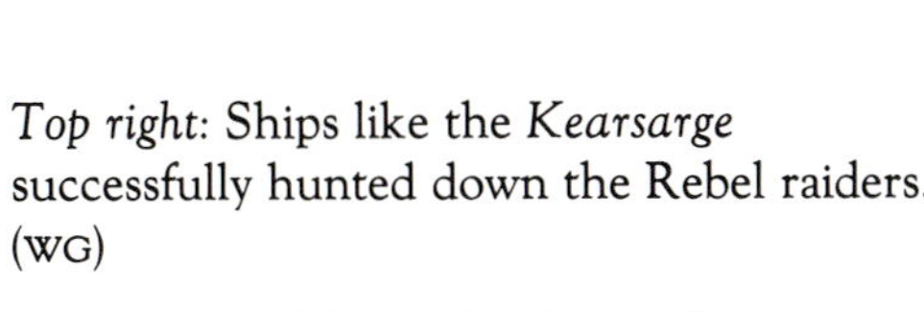

Top right: Ships like the *Kearsarge* successfully hunted down the Rebel raiders. (WG)

Bottom right: Men and officers of the *Kearsarge* pose with one of the guns on the quarterdeck just a few days after they met and sank the *Alabama* off Cherbourg, France, in June 1864. Their hunt, at last, was at an end. (USAMHI)

When not hunting prey, or carrying supplies, or polishing the brass and cleaning ship, the sailors of North and South lived much the same life. They loved to pose for the camera just as much as their comrades in the armies. Some even posed for "trick" images that showed the same man twice — like Joseph B. Upham, shown here as a civilian and as a first-assistant engineer. (USAMHI)

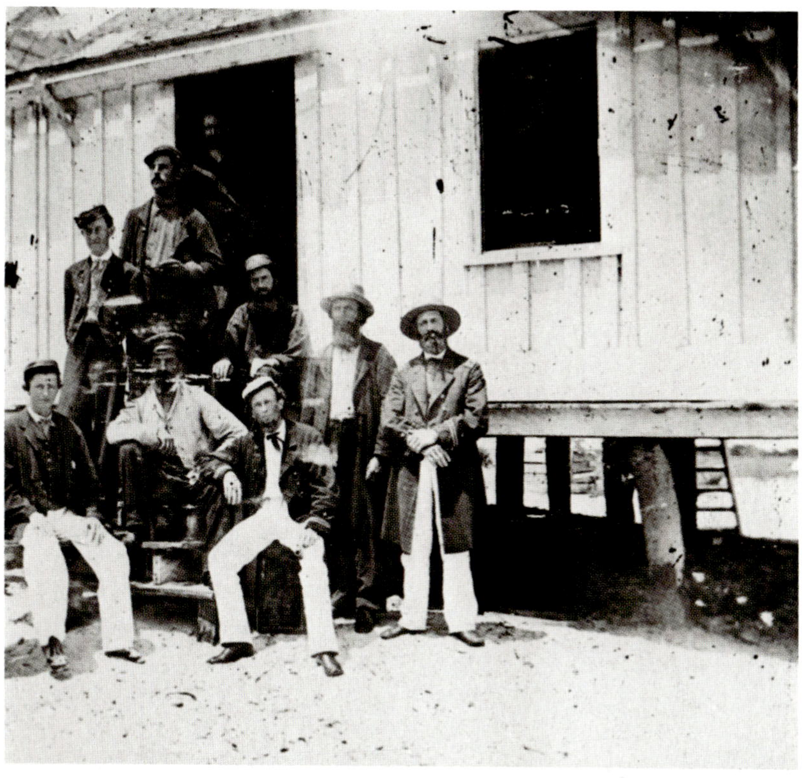

Wherever a camera appeared, so would they, even in front of a naval bakery. (USAMHI)

Posing for pictures was a welcome break from the routine of blockade or sea duty. (USAMHI)

And sitting for the camera gave the seamen a memento to remind them that in this war they, too, had done their part. (USAMHI)

Johnny Reb

A portfolio of the Confederate
fighting man in camp and field

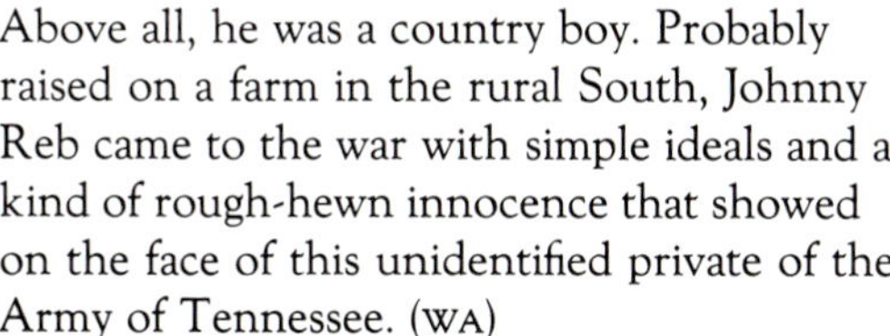

Above all, he was a country boy. Probably raised on a farm in the rural South, Johnny Reb came to the war with simple ideals and a kind of rough-hewn innocence that showed on the face of this unidentified private of the Army of Tennessee. (WA)

Top right: They flocked by tens of thousands to their banners in the early days of the war. Indeed, even before the firing on Fort Sumter, camps like those shown here at Pensacola, Florida, sprang from the Southern earth. J. D. Edwards of New Orleans was one of the few Southern photographers to take his camera outdoors to catch the look of the rustics in rebellion. This heretofore unpublished image taken from a lighthouse looks off toward the Warrington Navy Yard in the distance. (USAMHI)

Bottom right: Pensacola teemed with soldiers from Mississippi and Louisiana in the early months of 1861, Johnny Rebs anxious to stand in formation for Edwards's lens. (USAMHI)

Mississippi regiments encamped behind the lighthouse . . . (TU)

. . . and were delighted to line up for a pose. Uniforms for Johnny Reb were still more a dream than a reality in these early days. (LC)

Even the damage and fading of more than a century cannot dim the enthusiastic and determined stance of these Mississippians. (PHS)

Edwards captured a wonderful record of the look of Confederate soldiers in their camps. Later, with the Union blockade making photographic supplies scarce, it would have been almost impossible to record this scene of the Perote Guards as they self-consciously posed at camp chores and entertainments. (TU)

These men of the Ninth Mississippi display the wonderful variety of clothing that the boys took with them to war — some dressed for a day in the fields, others in formal attire, and a few in costumes seemingly drawn from comic opera. (RP)

Their tent streets were simple enough, with wooden and brush "shebangs" constructed to give shade from the hot sun. (USAMHI)

Probably a view of the Orleans Cadets from Louisiana, this Edwards image shows a wonderful variety of camp poses: lounging, bugling, fatigue duties, mock boxing, and an awkward corporal saluting an officer. (FSU)

A good game of cards was the best pastime of all. (RP)

In those pre-Sumter days, when there was no real shooting war yet, lounging and drilling were about all a Confederate had to do. Rebs like these Alabamians at Pensacola complained in their letters home that there would be no war for them to fight in. (LC)

Instead, they sat in their tents, read their books, wrote their letters, and mended their clothing, like these boys of the Ninth Mississippi's Company B, whom Edwards photographed during the war's first spring. (PHS)

Of course, there was plenty of work for the new Southern soldiers to do, wherever they were stationed. Though photographs survive from only Pensacola and a very few other places, the regimen was much the same everywhere. Daily parade and drill was inescapable, as it is here for the Orleans Cadets. (TU)

The Louisiana Zouaves were quartered here at the marine barracks in the Warrington Navy Yard, and they, too, can dimly be seen at parade in front of it. (TU)

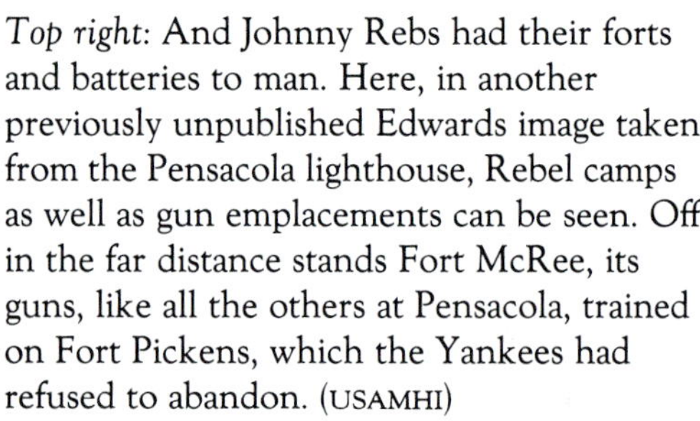

Top right: And Johnny Rebs had their forts and batteries to man. Here, in another previously unpublished Edwards image taken from the Pensacola lighthouse, Rebel camps as well as gun emplacements can be seen. Off in the far distance stands Fort McRee, its guns, like all the others at Pensacola, trained on Fort Pickens, which the Yankees had refused to abandon. (USAMHI)

Bottom right: These Confederates man a large battery in what is perhaps Fort Barrancas, an old earth and masonry stronghold outside Pensacola. Edwards's image, published here for the first time, shows the Rebs poised and ready—though, as it turned out, the guns they are manning were rarely fired during hostilities in the four-year war. (USAMHI)

But the Confederates were ready to fight if the war did come to them. This and several other Edwards images are no longer known to survive in the original, but old negative copies made in 1911 have recently come to light that allow a wonderful look at the poses, faces, and uniforms of these Southrons inside a well-manned water battery. (USAMHI)

Another of the newly discovered negatives shows the earth-covered bombproofs and dugout ammunition magazines that were intended to protect men and powder. With nothing but time on their hands, these Confederates — and thousands of others elsewhere throughout the war — spent a lot more time with spades in their hands than weapons. (USAMHI)

Sometimes one could only tell an officer by the shoulder straps hastily attached to his frock coat, as with the dapper fellow standing on the mortar carriage. In time, most Confederate units would become better uniformed, but there would always be a bewildering variety of headgear, shoes and boots, and equipment. (USAMHI)

No two hats are the same in this view of the same mortar, in which men have traded places to pose for Edwards. The lighthouse that afforded him panoramas of the area is visible in the background at left. (NA)

Top left: Wherever there was a cannon — like this ten-inch columbiad in a sand battery manned by the Perote Guards of Mississippi — young Rebs could be found to pose proudly for Edwards's camera. (PHS)

Top right: There were smiles, brandished swords, and an air of men who thought this war was going to be a lark, their only concern being that it might end before they got in a good lick at the Yanks. They would not be disappointed. (USAMHI)

Bottom right: Probably the most uniformly soldierly-looking Confederates that Edwards found were these Rebels manning Fort McRee. The fort itself has now all but vanished thanks to erosion, and the old image, too, no longer exists except in this long-lost 1911 copy negative. Happily, it still remains as testimony to the pioneering work of Edwards the photographer, and to the visage of Southern manhood in the first bright days of the war. (USAMHI)

J. W. Petty of Poydras Street in New Orleans was another pioneering artist who left behind a priceless record of the Rebels of '61. His series of images of New Orleans's famed Washington Artillery is the best record that has survived of a single Confederate unit in all its wonderful variety. Most of these images, too, were lost until recently. (USAMHI)

Just where Petty made his images is unknown, but probably it was while the unit was mustering before leaving New Orleans. Quarters were makeshift, to say the least. (USAMHI)

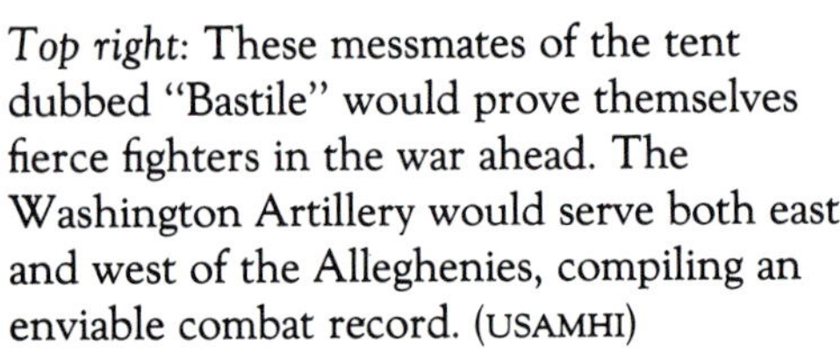

Top right: These messmates of the tent dubbed "Bastile" would prove themselves fierce fighters in the war ahead. The Washington Artillery would serve both east and west of the Alleghenies, compiling an enviable combat record. (USAMHI)

Bottom right: The calm of their pose belies their ferocity in battle. (USAMHI)

This group named its tent after the first Confederate victory in a land battle — Big Bethel, Virginia — which means that Petty's image must have been made after June 10, 1861. (USAMHI)

Harkening back to the days of the Revolution, several artillerists stand proudly at attention in front of "Lexington of '61." The Confederates all looked toward the Spirit of '76 for inspiration and example in their own revolution. (USAMHI)

Petty was apparently sufficiently taken with the striped tent of the boys of "Carondelet" that he . . . (CM)

. . . photographed them twice. Such a scene of luxury would be a real rarity two years hence in the Confederate army. (JPR)

It may have been Petty who photographed these men at Camp Lewis, near Carrollton, Louisiana. There were several companies of the Washington Artillery; these images show the Fifth Company. (CM)

Some of these Louisiana officers had a distinctly professorial look to them, yet the boys in the ranks came to love and respect them in time. They would follow them anywhere. (USAMHI)

"Dixie's Land" says the sign on the tent at right, and that was what all Confederates were fighting for. (USAMHI)

These Johnny Rebs called their home "Richmond Hill." Theirs are the faces of an innocent America about to grow up in a hurry. (USAMHI)

The lad at right might clown about, wearing a mess plate on his head, but a few years from now Johnny Reb would be fortunate to have such a dish, much less anything to put into it. (USAMHI)

Another famed Confederate unit named for the Father of His Country was the Washington Light Infantry of Charleston, South Carolina. No one knows who made a brief series of images of them in 1861. Here their officers stand before a tent brimming with equipment. (USAMHI)

Bottom left: A few of the boys sit in the shade . . . in full uniform. The truly "candid" pose seems not yet to have been invented. (USAMHI)

Bottom right: The "Music Hall" of the Washington Light Infantry could boast a fiddler or two and a bugler (leaning on his rifle, at left). Rebs took their songs with them wherever they went. (USAMHI)

And in the early days of the war, the more affluent took the luxuries of home with them, too, including their body servants, seen here about to serve their masters from ample picnic hampers. (WLI)

Many a Johnny Reb brought a slave to the war with him, and many of those slaves served faithfully throughout the war. Andrew Chandler sits below with his servant Silas. Before the war, many Southern states prohibited blacks from even carrying weapons. Now that had changed. (SC/RSY)

Less pretentious were these Texans, standing before their "Wigfall Mess" at Camp Quantico, Virginia. They would have to perform their own camp chores. (USAMHI)

Top right: More telling than anything else are the faces of Johnny Reb. (WA)

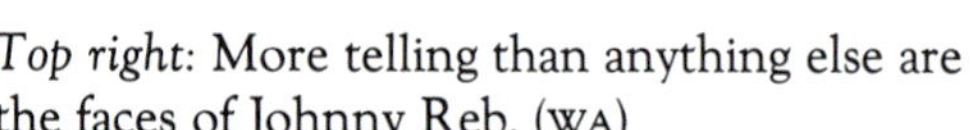

Bottom right: He loved the flag for which he fought, and upon which this bearded young Mars leans. (HP)

Like this Texan, Johnny Reb looked young for the most part, but the war aged him quickly. (WA)

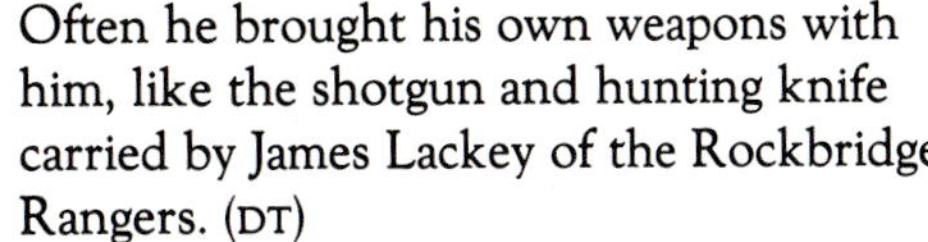

Often he brought his own weapons with him, like the shotgun and hunting knife carried by James Lackey of the Rockbridge Rangers. (DT)

He loved the flamboyant dress of the cavalryman. (HP)

Sometimes he looked more like a vestige of the Revolution, with an old flintlock rifle and a tricorn — like Thomas Gooch of Company C, Twentieth Mississippi. (MC)

When he could, Johnny Reb adopted the zouave and other forms of fancy uniform, even if he only wore it by half. (HP)

He armed himself to the teeth when he could. (WA)

What he lacked in worldly sophistication, he made up for in pure determination. (HP)

He went to war with his friends, to fight for them and his state. Two Virginians—Reggie T. Wingfield and Hamden T. Fay—sit for the camera. (JM)

They had a lot to give. (WA)

Most of all, like Sam Cocke, they gave their youth. (PC)

They went to war with antiquated weapons and dressed in homespun, like William Presgraves of Virginia, photographed on September 26, 1861. He would die the following year. (JAH)

And if they survived the storm at all, it would be as men — their boyhood, like their cause, lost forever. (PC)

A Yankee in Dixie
Baton Rouge Photographer A. D. Lytle

★

Charles East

FRANCIS TREVELYAN MILLER and the Review of Reviews Company editors who worked on the ten-volume *Photographic History of the Civil War* set out to cover the war from both sides, and in so doing to uncover images taken by Southern photographers whose work could stand alongside that of their Northern counterparts Mathew Brady, Alexander Gardner, and others. Publication of the commemorative volumes in 1911 was in fact an outgrowth of the movement toward reconciliation and reunion. Among the editors were two of the sons of the Southern poet Sidney Lanier, who had no doubt grown up with stories of their father's exploits as a Confederate signal officer and blockade-runner; among the contributors would be former Confederate officers, as well as the editor of the influential magazine *Confederate Veteran*, whose blessing was important to the success of the project.

The discovery that the Southern photographers were not adequately represented came as early as 1910, and we know from an obscure account of his travels through the South in the early months of 1911 that a former journalist and advertising man named Roy M. Mason was hired to visit Richmond, Charleston, Atlanta, and other cities in a last-minute effort to find the Southern Mathew Bradys. On February 12, 1911, Mason arrived in New Orleans and checked into his hotel. as he had done in a dozen other cities. He then made the rounds of the city's newspaper offices to inform the editors of his mission, and subsequently stories appeared in at least two of the papers.

Someone in Baton Rouge, upriver from New Orleans, saw one of the newspaper stories and wrote a postcard addressed to Mason at the Saint Charles Hotel, saying that he had Civil War naval photographs. Mason immediately took the train to Baton Rouge, but discovered that the "photographs" were "woodcuts, copies, engravings, only one original, which I borrowed. But," Mason recalled, "he told me that A. D. Lytle, a local photographer, had some photographs. I called, and found a veritable mine. Lytle had been a Confederate spy, and had sent through to the Confederate secret service photographs of every camp, battery, regiment, headquarters and lookout tower of the Union army of General [Nathaniel P.] Banks, and of [David D.] Porter's and [David G.] Farragut's fleet upon the Mississippi."

Lytle still had all the glass negatives, but no one in Baton Rouge would undertake to make prints from them for Mason in less than a week. "The photographer demanded a large sum for his treasures, and I wired to the powers that were. The sum arrived, and I departed with the drama of the Red River and Port Hudson expeditions on glass plates in my arms." Mason goes on to tell how he had prints made from the Lytle negatives while in New Orleans and then sent the prints and plates to the Review of Reviews offices in New York. "I returned once more to Baton Rouge to get all the data I could in regard to the Lytle photographs, and then went up the Mississippi to Natchez and Vicksburg."

Mason's excitement over the discovery of the Lytle photographs was obviously communicated to the editors in New York, and when the ten-volume work was published at the end of the year and in the early months of 1912, the name A. D. Lytle for the first time entered the history of American photography. At least eleven of Lytle's photographs were reproduced in the first volume — one of these a wartime photograph of his Baton Rouge gallery, which shares a page with the famous full-figure portrait of Mathew Brady in linen duster, "just returned from Bull Run." Throughout the work over fifty of his images appear, more generous treatment than any of the other Southern photographers received.

The Lytle photographs show a small city in the lower South, the state's capital until 1861, at an extraordinary time in its history. First occupied by the enemy army in May 1862, and under the guns of the Federal fleet from then until the end of the war, Baton Rouge early in 1863 became the staging area and hospital for the Federal campaign against nearby Port Hudson, and a base of operations for General Banks's ill-fated drive up the Red River the year following.

Most of the wartime views that we can identify as being his seem to have been taken in either the spring or summer of 1862 (the first period of Union occupation) or between December 1862 (when the city was reoccupied) and July 1863 (the surrender of Port Hudson). What we see are cavalry camps, public buildings used to quarter troops or to serve as makeshift hospitals, soldiers standing at parade, officers seated amid their tents at posed leisure — and a vast array of naval vessels, from monster ironclads and the smaller tinclads to Porter's flotilla of mortar boats waiting to be towed to positions just outside the range of Confederate guns along the bluffs at Port Hudson.

One interesting aspect of Lytle's career and his subsequent placement among great Southern photographers — and this is also true of the New Orleans photographer J. D. Edwards — is that he was Northern-born and only on the eve of the war could claim to be a Southerner. Lytle had traveled through the South taking pictures in the late 1850s and had spent several months of 1859 in Baton Rouge, but it is doubtful that he decided to locate there permanently until 1860, when he advertised in one of the local papers for "a small house with three or four rooms, in a central part of town." Any person having such a house, he said, "can find a good paying tenant."

Andrew David Lytle was born in Deerfield, in Warren County, Ohio, April 4, 1834, the son of David Lytle, a tanner. Not long after his father's death in 1838, young Andrew's mother, Dorcas Mounts Lytle, married a man named John Waldron, who died a little over a year later. By 1850 the widowed Dorcas Waldron was living in Cincinnati with her four children, one of them sixteen-year-old Andrew. On June 20, 1855, Andrew married Mary Ann Lundy, whose father was an engraver and a manufacturer of gold pens, and at about this time, if not earlier, he began his apprenticeship under one of the Cincinnati photographers, possibly the well-known daguerreotypist William S. Porter. In 1856 Lytle was working as a daguerreotypist at 83 West Fourth Street — the same address as that given for Porter.

During the 1850s Lytle joined two military organizations that may have been as much social as military, and in one — the Rover Cadets — he held the rank of captain, a title that seems to have stuck with him. He began to travel through the Southern states as a photographer even before he left Cincinnati, and after two years of such traveling, in 1857, he located at Baton Rouge. The earliest actual record of his having been in the city is an advertisement that appeared in one of the Baton Rouge newspapers on December 18, 1858, announcing that "the World Renowned Artists LYTLE & GIBSON, have arrived in our city, and taken Rooms in Heroman's Brick Block, where they are prepared to execute work in the various branches of the PHOTOGRAPHIC ART. They also make the celebrated LYTLEOTYPE, which is made by them only."

It is clear that Lytle and his partner, whose first name is unknown, were itinerants — two in a succession of traveling photographers who passed through Baton Rouge from time to time before 1860. They occupied a gallery on the upper floor of the three-story Heroman Building, the newest and finest building of its kind in the city, and their popularity may have kept them longer than they had intended. The *Daily Advocate* reported that their rooms were "crowded every day, with the elite and fashion of our city, to procure one of their highly celebrated pictures, made of glass, iron and paper." In April and May of 1859, Lytle and Gibson advertised that they would shortly be leaving, and they were gone by the middle of June — off for Mississippi, where they said they would remain for the summer.

The death of the Lytles' two-year-old son Andrew David Lytle, Jr., occurred during their stay in the city, and it is possible that one of the reasons why they decided to settle in Baton Rouge rather than in some other city is that the little boy was buried there.

Lytle returned to Baton Rouge in the fall. In the November 18, 1859, issue of the *Daily Gazette & Comet,* "Lytle & Co." announced that they were located on Main Street across from the Harney House hotel, and this is the location where Lytle continued to operate a gallery for more than fifty years. It occupied the second floor of a building on the south side of Main, only a block or so from the levee and the river.

There was one more departure for Mississippi in June of the following year, but Lytle was back in Baton Rouge by August — and, advertising for a house for himself. It would be a few years more before he and his wife owned their own home on the Boulevard, not far from the governor's mansion. The events that were about to engulf them would be catastrophic, but they did not know it. The victory of Lincoln in the November 1860 presidential election set the stage for the secession of Louisiana and the other Southern states, the formation of the Confederacy, and the war that was to follow.

In Baton Rouge the gathering of first the legislature and then the secession convention kept Lytle busy with his portrait work, which was always the bread and butter of his photography business. As the excitement mounted and the city teemed with young men organizing themselves into military companies like the Baton Rouge Fencibles and the Pelican Rifles, he was even busier, according to the columns of the local newspapers. "Lytle's Gallery is crowded every day with 'our boys' getting their pictures before leaving for the wars," the *Daily Advocate* reported not long after the opening shots at Fort Sumter. Apparently, when the war came Lytle employed his experience with the Rover Cadets in drilling two or three companies for the Confederate service. He held no rank in the Confederate army, and neither did the men he was drilling, though the local militia companies were later mustered into Confederate service.

In the first year of the war, many of those who came to Lytle's gallery to have their pictures taken were young men about to be soldiers, or soldiers wearing their first uniforms and about to go aboard a steamboat headed upriver to Vicksburg and Memphis or downriver to New Orleans — sons of the Confederacy. With the arrival of Farragut's fleet and the occupation of Baton Rouge by troops under the command of Brig. Gen. Thomas Williams in May 1862, the officers and men — and gunboats and guns — of the Union army and navy became his subjects. Most of the white families of the city fled in the summer of 1862 and did not come back to claim their homes and pick up their lives until the end of the war. Lytle, however, remained — or if he left, was gone only briefly. He continued to operate his gallery through the period of the occupation, and when the war was over he quickly established himself as a leading citizen of Baton Rouge and the city's premier photographer. When Roy Mason came upon him in 1911, Lytle was in his mid-seventies and his health was failing, though he was to live for another six years. The old man died on the afternoon of June 8, 1917, at his home on the Boulevard; his wife had died nineteen years earlier.

The recognition that came to Lytle in his old age with the publication of the *Photographic History of the Civil War* was deserved attention, but it has been clouded by the question of Lytle's supposed role as a Confederate secret-service agent, or, as Henry Wysham Lanier called him in a preface to the ten volumes, a "camera spy" for the Confederacy. In the opening pages of the first volume, under a photograph of the First Indiana Heavy Artillery at Baton Rouge that is identified as having been taken by Lytle, the caption reads: "With a courage and skill as remarkable as that of Brady himself this Confederate photographer risked his life to obtain negatives of Federal batteries, cavalry regiments and camps, lookout towers, and the vessels of Farragut and Porter, in fact of everything that might be of the slightest use in informing the Confederate Secret Service of the strength of the Federal occupation of Baton Rouge." The caption writer, who may have been Mason, added: "In Lytle's little shop on Main Street these negatives remained in oblivion for near half a century," until they were "unearthed by the editors of the 'Photographic History.'"

In his preface Lanier tells us that Lytle took "a series of views . . . for the specific use of the Confederate Secret Service," explains how the photographer was able to obtain his chemicals during wartime, and introduces another element to the story: "Mr. Lytle's son relates that his father used to signal with flag and lantern from the observation tower on the top of the ruins of the Baton Rouge capitol to Scott's Bluff, whence the messages were relayed to the Confederates near New Orleans; but he found this provided such a tempting target for the Federal sharpshooters that he discontinued the practice." References to Lytle in several of the subsequent volumes give essentially the same information.

Lanier's mention of Lytle's son Howard as a source presents the possibility that information concerning his father's role as a Confederate secret agent originated with Howard and not with his father. On the other hand, Howard's story of his father's having signaled from the observation tower atop the fire-gutted State House (the building burned the night of December 28, 1862) may simply have been a postscript or addendum to the story that the old man himself had already told: of his having passed photographs along to the Confederates. In other words, one may have been only incidental to the other. The sense of Mason's account is that he met and talked with Lytle—that it was the photographer himself who "demanded a large sum for his treasures." Roy Mason never mentions Howard Lytle, though Mason must surely be the source for Lanier's statement; and, given the fact that Howard and his father were close and worked out of the same gallery (by now A. D. Lytle & Son), it seems likely that Howard was present on the occasion of both of Mason's visits.

The truth about what role, if any, the Baton Rouge photographer played as a Confederate secret agent has never been—and may never be—determined. Those who reject the story out of hand can cite the absence of evidence that Lytle served in any Confederate unit, though that, given the circumstances of the time and place, is hardly conclusive. Another argument, that Lytle's photographs would have been of little use to the Confederates—would have told them nothing more than they could have learned otherwise—is a retrospective one. We know a great deal more about military intelligence than was known in 1862 and 1863, and it is clear both from the official correspondence and from other sources that as the Union army and navy converged on Port Hudson in the early months of 1863, the Confederates were grasping for information—and had set up a rather extensive network for gathering it. The signal stations strung along the Mississippi River for some twenty-five miles, from Baton Rouge to Port Hudson (the one nearest Baton Rouge on the east bank of the river was very likely at Scott's Bluff), were only a part of their operations.

The officer in charge of Confederate Signal Corps operations in the vicinity of Baton Rouge in the early months of 1863 was Capt. J. W. Youngblood, who reported directly to Maj. Gen. Franklin Gardner, the officer in command at Port Hudson. Gardner in turn relayed the information to his superiors. "I have reliable information from Baton Rouge" is a phrase that recurred in Gardner's official correspondence, as he awaited the coming of the Union army then gathering in the former capital. The Signal Corps unit was rather amorphous in nature. In addition to those assigned to the unit, there were also those whose status was no more than quasi-official, as well as others who remained civilians. When, in July, they learned that General Gardner had surrendered Port Hudson, many of them simply faded away. Thus, they were not among those surrendered.

It is in this context that Lytle may have turned over photographs to someone with the intention of their being used by the Confederates. It may have been someone attached to the Signal Corps in either an official or an unofficial capacity. It may have been a civilian. Whoever it was, the best guess is that the Signal Corps was the channel. There is, as a matter of fact, one sentence in a biographical sketch of Lytle published in 1892 that lends credence to the theory. This is not necessarily Lytle himself speaking, but it must surely be an account drawn from information supplied by him; and what it tells us is that he "attached himself to the Confederate Signal service, with which he was connected at the fall of Port Hudson." Lytle's connection with what the sketch calls the Confederate Signal service is almost certainly the basis for the story that resurfaced twenty years later in the *Photographic History*.

The question of whether Lytle was a secret agent, whether he worked with or for the Confederate Signal Corps or the secret service, will continue to intrigue us, but it should not divert us. What is important about Lytle — the reason he merits our attention — is that he was there when the war came to his particular corner of the Confederacy, that he took the pictures — and, of course, that he kept them, until the day when someone like Roy Mason came climbing the stairs to his gallery.

The waterfront of Baton Rouge, with the Louisiana State House standing at far right. Like all of the images in this chapter, this photograph is reproduced from a print made directly from A. D. Lytle's newly discovered glass-plate negatives. (USAMHI)

A street scene in Baton Rouge, perhaps before a parade or some other public festivity, as whites and blacks line both sides of the road. The artist signed his own work here, "Lytle, Photographist." (USAMHI)

Even though a state capital in time of war, Baton Rouge was a quiet town as captured on Lytle's plates. (USAMHI)

Tree-lined side streets and picket fences led the way between the public buildings and to and from the river. (USAMHI)

The State House, built in the 1840s, dominated the small city. (USAMHI)

The substantial home of Samuel M. Hart on Church Street gives little evidence of the service it later saw as headquarters for a Yankee general. (USAMHI)

Lytle liked to take his camera up to Baton Rouge's high places, usually church steeples, to capture his elevated views of the city. (USAMHI)

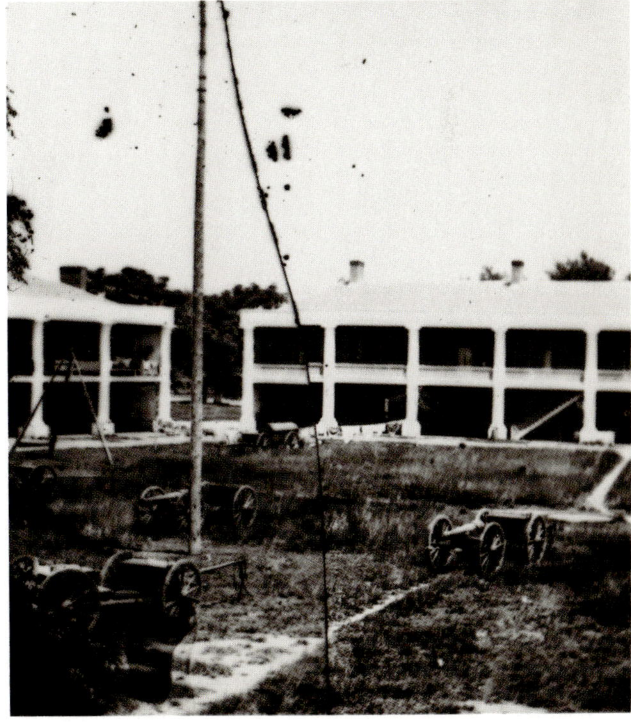

Another of his favorite subjects was the Baton Rouge Barracks, looking a bit disheveled here with the laundry hanging out to dry. (USAMHI)

Top left: Lytle liked the private dwellings, too, many of which were occupied by Federal officers after the city fell to the Yankees. (USAMHI)

Top right: Most of all, he turned his camera toward evidences of the war that had swept the city. All around the fringes there were camps of laborers and soldiers. (USAMHI)

Many of Baton Rouge's homes and businesses were burned when the Yankee commanders needed to clear a path between the city and the river for their artillery. This was one of the saddest images to come before Lytle's lens. (USAMHI)

The Yankees had come by the river, and, inevitably, Lytle devoted most of his plates to the ribbon of water that brought the war to Baton Rouge. Adm. David G. Farragut's flagship *Hartford* is believed to be the vessel lying off Main Street. (USAMHI)

The waterfront would be jammed with naval hardware and refuse for years. (USAMHI)

And always the gunboats lay at their moorings on the bank. Two mortar schooners sit at right, while at far left rests the wooden gunboat *Tyler*, its starboard stack a bit awry. (USAMHI)

There were regular commercial steamboats — packets — coming and going. (USAMHI)

But Lytle's real interest was the warships. Here what is believed to be Farragut's *Hartford* rests at anchor out in the stream. (USAMHI)

One of the workhorse "woodclads" of the river fleet, the *Conestoga.* (USAMHI)

A host of other gunboats, called tinclads because of their light armor, went up and down the river and paused for Lytle's camera. Most had names, but for some only numbers are known — like the No. 53. (USAMHI)

There was little uniformity among the tinclads, since many were simply prewar river steamers converted to military use. No. 8 was seen all up and down the Mississippi. (USAMHI)

This one, its number indistinguishable, bore a combination of straight and sloping sides, with a rounded bow and only half a cabin deck. (USAMHI)

A perfect example of an ersatz tinclad, this unidentified vessel actually has two turrets, one fore and the other aft. The ship fairly bristles with guns. (USAMHI)

Bottom left: Farragut's fleet included more conventional ships like the *Albatross* . . . (USAMHI)

Bottom right: . . . and even a few captured Confederate ships, most notably the *General Sterling Price.* Seized in 1862, this vessel somehow captivated Lytle's imagination, for he made more images of it than of any other ship. (USAMHI)

Top left: The *Conestoga* rests aft of the *Price* in this image. A few weeks after this photograph was made, the *Price* accidentally rammed and sank the other ship. (USAMHI)

Top right: The ram *Defender* was often mistaken for the *Price*. Its job was a simple one: to sink its reinforced prow into an enemy hull. (USAMHI)

This is believed to be the artillery transport that carried Gen. Thomas Williams's body away from Baton Rouge after he fell in the August 5, 1862, battle. The photograph was presumably taken after the ship was sunk by the Confederates and subsequently raised. (USAMHI)

Here another Civil War innovation, the hospital ship, stands for Lytle just aft of the *Price*. This one is the *Red Rover*, a captured Rebel transport. (USAMHI)

There were great leviathans in the Yankee fleet for Lytle to look upon. The USS *Essex* was one of the earliest and largest major ironclads on the river. (USAMHI)

Bottom left: The huge USS *Choctaw* was even larger, and more dreadful-looking. Her mammoth sidewheels and towering twin smokestacks dwarfed the single-stacked tinclad at her aft. (USAMHI)

Bottom right: Mounting relatively few guns, but of high caliber, she looked virtually invincible. (USAMHI)

Equally formidable was the *Lafayette*. Lytle never tired of pointing his lens toward these ungainly engines of war. (USAMHI)

The men who served these warships also interested him. This group of seven naval officers is unidentified, though they appear to be aboard one of the tinclads. (USAMHI)

The name of their ship, *Choctaw*, appears on the hatbands of some of these sailors, photographed aboard the vessel. (USAMHI)

Some of his photographs, like this other view of the *Choctaw*'s sailors, Lytle may have printed in quantity to sell as souvenirs. (USAMHI)

Lytle did a brisk portrait business, with studio poses like this one of Brig. Gen. Joseph Bailey, who appears to be wearing a mourning badge on his left arm, perhaps indicating that the image was made at war's end after the murder of Lincoln. (USAMHI)

Or like this fine portrait of Brig. Gen. Edward J. Davis. (USAMHI)

Some of those Lytle photographed are lost to history. This brigadier defies positive identification. (USAMHI)

As does this one — though he might be William P. Benton, who stayed in the South after the war and died in New Orleans's tragic yellow-fever epidemic of 1867. (USAMHI)

Benton — or whoever he may be — poses with fellow officers for Lytle. (USAMHI)

General Bailey and fellow officers pose in a rare interior setting. (USAMHI)

Lytle even tried mass-producing souvenir photos for the Yankees who came to Baton Rouge. He made photographic montages of portraits of all the officers of regiments, like the First Indiana Heavy Artillery . . . (USAMHI)

. . . and the Ninety-second United States Colored Troops. These could sell in large quantity, and help subsidize the photographer's passion for recording Baton Rouge's war on glass. (USAMHI)

Judging from this beautiful portrait of Confederate colonel Randall L. Gibson, it would appear that Lytle managed to work his lens early in the war, before the Rebels lost Baton Rouge. Yet very few of his Confederate portraits are known to survive. (USAMHI)

A few of Lytle's images would become almost famous, and none more so than this winter 1862/63 picture of the camps of the Seventh Vermont and Twenty-first Indiana. It is perhaps the finest image in existence of Yankee camps in the South. (USAMHI)

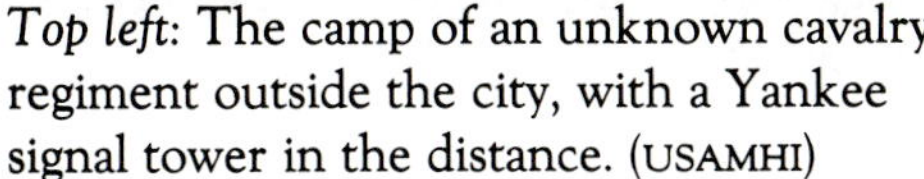

Top left: The camp of an unknown cavalry regiment outside the city, with a Yankee signal tower in the distance. (USAMHI)

Top right: Lytle seems to have often posed his outdoor views with some landmark in the background, usually the State House, which here rises behind the winter quarters of an unknown Yankee regiment. (USAMHI)

The smoke rising from campfires marks yet another Federal camp. Like their Confederate enemies, the Yanks, too, erected shebangs of brush to protect themselves from the merciless Southern sun. (USAMHI)

Lytle's camera caught Federal camps stretching to every point of the compass from Baton Rouge. (USAMHI)

Lytle made a beautiful image of Massachusetts's artillery posing before the Baton Rouge Barracks. He seems to have had no problem persuading these Yankees to hold still for his camera. (USAMHI)

Another of Lytle's more famous images is this one of the First Indiana Heavy Artillery. It has long been supposed to have been taken in his presumed secret-service capacity for the Confederacy, though that would seem suspect. The South did not need Lytle's photographs to know what a Yankee battery looked like. (USAMHI)

Another of the supposed secret-service images of the First Indiana. In fact, to today's eye, there appears to be little, if any, useful military information to be found in it. (USAMHI)

The Louisiana State Penitentiary shares the plate with the First Wisconsin Light Artillery in one of Lytle's finer unit pictures. (USAMHI)

Lytle liked group images of the Federal soldiers who filled Baton Rouge's streets, and he often made portraits of smart-looking outfits like this one posing before the courthouse where they may have been quartered. (USAMHI)

Yet another view of troops in front of the courthouse. (USAMHI)

Outside the city, Lytle caught this image of a company of the Thirteenth Connecticut. (USAMHI)

Three Yankee officers and a civilian lounge before a tent whose well-equipped interior includes even an étagère, probably liberated from some Baton Rouge home. (USAMHI)

Maj. Gen. Christopher C. Augur sits in a rocking chair to the left of his fellow officers, amid a uniquely military display in the campsite garden. (USAMHI)

One thing that Lytle's camera preserved most of all was the fact that life, even amid war, went on in Baton Rouge. Here he caught a bandwagon out politicking for a state senatorial candidate. (USAMHI)

And here, on the grounds of the old state arsenal, his lens offered testimony to the end of the war at last, as the photographer surveyed the captured artillery of the final Confederate army east of the Mississippi to surrender. (USAMHI)

Seventeen years later, Lytle was still in Baton Rouge, recording the return of one of the most famous veterans of the war on the Mississippi: the 1882 visit of the refitted *Hartford*. Truly, A. D. Lytle and his camera were a unique partnership in their witness to war. (USAMHI)

The Men Who Led

Richard J. Sommers

In war, men are nothing; *the* man is everything." So said Napoleon, thinking of himself as "*the* man" who inspirited and directed the war. He exaggerated, of course. Yet leadership unquestionably is crucial to war: if not leadership by one emperor-commander, then collective command by all the men who led.

Certainly this was true of the Civil War. Command very much remained a subjective art practiced by the commander himself, aided only by a tiny staff and untrammeled by modern staff planners, resource managers, and detailed doctrines. And those commanders were leaders. In camp, march, and especially battle, they set examples to give their troops tone, courage, and inspiration.

Such leadership particularly prevailed at intermediate command levels. Commanders' basic administrative unit was the regiment. Numbering 1,000 to 1,200 men at full strength, entirely of one combat arm (infantry, cavalry, light or heavy artillery, or engineers), most regiments were raised by states or territories, then mustered into national service. They bore state names and numerical designations by state and branch of service. In contrast to thousands of these state volunteer units, both national governments directly raised barely 150 volunteer regiments, mostly Negro; and the Federal regular army was tiny, the Confederate regular army minuscule.

Almost all troops thus were not career men but citizen-soldiers who enlisted only for the war. At regimental level, so were their leaders. Admittedly, many former professional soldiers initially rejoined the army as colonels commanding state regiments. Even future army commanders U. S. Grant (Twenty-first Illinois), Samuel R. Curtis (Second Iowa), and John B. Hood (Fourth Texas) briefly led regiments. Again, in mid-1862, the U.S. War Department finally authorized regular officers leave to command volunteers. Adelbert Ames (Twentieth Maine) and Eli Long (Fourth Ohio Cavalry) were among those thus transferring, but many soon received higher command and rank.

Most leaders remaining with regiments were not such ex-regulars but citizen-soldiers like their men. Many colonels, indeed, helped raise the regiments they were then elected or appointed to command. These inexperienced commanders sometimes proved inept and resigned or were forced out. Yet, overall, they deserve praise, not scorn. There were not enough regulars for all command positions, so who could better fill those offices than lawyers, bankers, teachers, politicians—leaders from civil life from whom their citizen-soldiers customarily sought guidance? This was America's historical militia system of republics, and it continued working reasonably well in the Civil War. If not always initially, then later, through the crucible of war itself, able leaders rose to command regiments. Some of these citizen-colonels of 1861, indeed, earned corps command by 1864: Northerners John A. Logan, John M. Palmer, Alfred H. Terry, and Francis P. Blair, Jr.; Southerners John C. Breckinridge, Nathan Bedford Forrest, Wade Hampton, and John B. Gordon.

Promotion came more often to leaders tabbed for brigade command, as regiments were marshaled into armies in 1861. These were the more promising regular officers and the more influential civil leaders. Much was expected of them, and many subsequently achieved high command, if not always high success. Of the approximately 130 Federal and Confederate brigadier generals in 1861, 38 became army or department commanders, including Yankees George G. Meade, Edward Ord, William S. Rosecrans, George H. Thomas, and Benjamin F. Butler, and Secessionists Thomas J. ("Stonewall") Jackson, James Longstreet, Edmund Kirby Smith, Theophilus H. Holmes, and Richard S. Ewell. Resignation, removal, illness, or casualty eliminated others. Only 5 of those early brigadiers remained at that level in 1865.

Combat caused much such attrition, for brigades were the chess pieces of battle, the units of tactical maneuver. Brigadiers led those pieces into the fray to set examples and keep at least some control. The maelstrom of war marked some for promotion, others for removal, still others for disablement or death. Mortality rates were frightful. Of 583 Northern generals, 47 were killed in battle, 27 at brigade level—among them Joshua Sill, Strong Vincent, and Hiram Burnham. Confederate casualties were even worse: 77 of 425 generals were slain, 53 of them brigadiers, like George Doles, John Gregg, and States Rights Gist. Adding those colonels killed while commanding brigades heightens the attrition rate, especially for Yankees. Whereas the South usually conferred rank commensurate with office, the Union, from midwar onward, consistently lagged one rank below office. Over 40 Federal colonels were killed at the head of brigades, even divisions, to which they had not yet been promoted.

Not rank but role defined a brigade: its tactical function and the manpower to accomplish it. Cavalry and artillery were peripheral to battle. Improvements in weapons and tactics largely banished cavalry from battlefields until late war. Rather than group horsemen with infantry, cavalry stayed separate in small brigades of three to five regiments to guard, screen, pursue, and raid. Artillery, in contrast, served with infantry, but experience soon suggested that, instead of one battery per brigade, cannons functioned better when controlled at higher levels. Graycoats combined batteries into an artillery battalion of three to six companies per infantry division, and Unionists grouped batteries into an artillery brigade of four to fourteen companies per corps.

Artillery supported, and cavalry screened, but the burden of fighting remained with the infantry. Brigades 3,000 to 4,000 strong were adequate for such fighting and were about as much as one leader could control in the confusion of combat. Secessionists needed only four or five regiments to achieve such strength, for individual replacements joined existing regiments, thus enabling recruits to benefit from serving alongside veterans and enabling each regiment to maintain strength. Except when casualties were annihilating, as at Spotsylvania and Nashville, or home-state recruiting bases were inaccessible (for Texans serving in Georgia, for instance), Southerners preserved regimental strength reasonably well until the last two years of the war.

The North, too, sent replacements to existing regiments, but it raised manpower principally by creating new ones: big, bright—and inexperienced. Casualties and illness eroded old regiments down to 100 to 200 men, but political reality precluded eliminating those state outfits except when enlistments expired. Maintaining a brigade at desired strength often required eight to twelve little regiments. Sometimes regimental attrition forced divisions, corps, even whole armies to reduce to more realistic size. Adding new regiments to brigades was what enabled divisions and corps to become leaner. This Union system of recruiting and replacement was clearly inferior to the South's. It was the fundamental disparity in *overall* manpower, not the system mobilizing it, which offset that Northern disadvantage.

Another difference — this one's benefit less clear-cut — was that Secessionists, with their heritage of states' rights, intentionally brigaded regiments by state. Although, on each side, the national government, not states, created brigades, the Confederacy by 1862 arranged for each brigade, whenever possible, to contain regiments from only one state. The North, however, with its broader outlook, usually brigaded together regiments from different states. While one-state Federal brigades did exist, much commoner were brigades with regiments from four or five states, especially as tiny regiments were grouped into big brigades in 1863 and 1864. With such diversity, Yankee brigades lacked the state pride of Butternut brigades, but the forge of battle soon kindled within Northern soldiers intense loyalty to their own brigade, however cosmopolitan its composition.

This state-versus-national focus found its counterpart among brigadiers. In both armies, regular and volunteer generals were presidential appointees. Only militia generals were appointed by state governors. Rarely did Union militia generals take the field. Emergencies requiring militia occurred more often in the invaded Confederacy.

Even among Secessionists, though, volunteer generals leading volunteer troops did most fighting. Yet President Jefferson Davis usually appointed Confederate brigadiers from the same state as their respective brigades. Doing otherwise provoked outbursts from state governors and legislators. Fewer such problems troubled President Abraham Lincoln. Although he shrewdly apportioned appointees among states, he needed not assign them to state brigades since the North had few such units.

In 1861, Davis and Secretary of War Judah Benjamin favored extending state homogeneity to the next command level: divisions. Generals P. G. T. Beauregard and Joseph E. Johnston, however, dissuaded them for fear that disaster to such a division would ravage the given state's manpower. Of all infantry divisions in the two main Confederate armies, just George Pickett's Virginians *after* Gettysburg and Benjamin F. Cheatham's Tennesseans intermittently throughout the war came exclusively from one state. Only the relatively quiescent Trans-Mississippi Army was, by 1864, completely organized into infantry divisions by states: three from Texas, one each from Louisiana, Arkansas, and Missouri.

In contrast, Bluecoats, with few state brigades, had fewer state divisions. Even these, moreover, were usually short-lived. Ironically, the Civil War's most famous state division wore blue: the Pennsylvania Volunteer Reserve Corps. Successively under George A. McCall, John F. Reynolds, Meade, and Samuel W. Crawford, it repeatedly saw heavy fighting, from 1861 to 1864.

Whether from one state or many, divisions served as units of tactical control. With primitive communications over far-flung, often wooded battlefields, a division could rarely attack en masse. Division commanders instead maneuvered brigades, which did the actual fighting. Light cavalry divisions usually contained two brigades if Southern and three if Northern, whereas heavy infantry divisions in the Confederate army generally numbered four to six brigades, as opposed to three or four in the Federal army.

Controlling so many brigades in battle required not just bravery but also tactical skill. Each side exercised particular care in selecting promising veterans, usually regulars, to lead divisions. Forty-one such Yankees headed divisions when the armies began moving in March of 1862. Some, like William T. Sherman, Fighting Joe Hooker, and George Thomas, became army commanders. Others, like Silas Casey, Alexander Asboth, and Benjamin Prentiss, were soon shunted aside. The majority rose at least to corps command, but, overall, that initial group proved disappointing — not in terms of competence, but in their mediocrity. Only the winnowing experience of war brought to the top the promising brigadiers, colonels, and captains — like Charles Griffin, Romeyn B. Ayres, William B.

Hazen, Joseph A. Mower — who so graced Northern division command by 1865.

Gray divisional generals shone right from the start. Some, admittedly, were inept, like George B. Crittenden and Benjamin Huger, but most were outstanding commanders. Spring 1862 saw among Southern division commanders Stonewall Jackson, James Longstreet, Richard Ewell, D. H. Hill, and William J. Hardee. Soon rising to that level were A. P. Hill, Richard H. Anderson, Jubal A. Early, Patrick R. Cleburne, and John S. Bowen. As promotion and attrition subsequently created vacancies, able officers like Robert E. Rodes, Joseph B. Kershaw, and Edward C. Walthall received divisions. Throughout the war, Confederate armies drew strength, leadership, and cohesion from a good, solid group of division commanders. This was especially true in Virginia, considerably true in Tennessee through Georgia, and less so in Mississippi and the Trans-Mississippi — which is not coincidental, for many officers who had fallen short in the East, like Theophilus Holmes and William W. Loring, were reassigned west of the great river.

Divisions, like brigades and regiments, were traditional American military organizations. Union general in chief Winfield Scott, indeed, initially organized armies on the pattern he used so successfully in Mexico in 1847. In March 1862, however, each side introduced a higher formation, created by Napoleon in 1805 but new to Americans: the corps. That month, the Federal Army of the Potomac was organized into five corps, and the Confederate Army of the Mississippi was grouped into four corps. By January 1863, all major armies had adopted corps structure.

The Butternuts eventually created nineteen infantry corps and nine cavalry corps, numbered in respect to each army. There were thus five "I Corps," corresponding to five armies. The North initially followed that pattern but in autumn of 1862 began redesignating corps in respect to the armed might of the Union. Hence, there was only one "I Corps," which happened to serve in the Army of the Potomac. Other early I Corps were renumbered XI, XIII, and XX. Altogether, the Bluecoats had thirty-six infantry corps, numbered I through XXV, with numbers from some deactivated corps reassigned to new corps. There were also seven cavalry corps.

These corps contained anywhere from two to six divisions, but usually three or four. In 1862, a cavalry regiment or brigade sometimes served with an infantry corps. Experience, however, taught each side not to fragment its horsemen but to concentrate them into their own divisions or corps. That year, Jeb Stuart, Joe Wheeler, and Earl Van Dorn led big Gray cavalry divisions, expanded into corps in 1863. In 1863 also, Northerners began forming cavalry corps under George Stoneman and David S. Stanley. Only then did Federal mounted units come into their own.

Cavalry corps could raid, screen, pursue, and fight. They not only fought each other but also engaged on borders of battlefields and increasingly on battlefields themselves — not with outmoded mounted saber charges but with dismounted carbine fire, often with repeaters. Infantry corps, however, were too big to fight tactically. They instead provided grand tactical and tactical control: the maneuvering of divisions up to, onto, and on battlefields. In broader panorama, moreover, corps served as army commanders' chess pieces of strategic maneuver, just as brigades were division commanders' battle chess pieces.

Controlling grand tactics and maneuvering with strategic latitude required great initiative, ability, and judgment. For his seven corps, Napoleon selected his most promising generals and made them marshals. Neither in rank nor ability did the first eight Union corps commanders equal Napoleonic precedent. Irvin McDowell, Edwin V. Sumner, Samuel P. Heintzelman, Erasmus D. Keyes, Nathaniel P. Banks, Alexander M. McCook, Charles C. Gilbert, and Thomas L. Crittenden were variously ill-starred, overrated, inept, or mediocre. By autumn 1863 only influential politician Banks retained major command at the front. War's winnowing influence eliminated the others and elevated abler men. Whether regulars like A. J. Smith, politicians like John Logan, or cavalrymen like James H. Wilson, Federal corps commanders by 1864 were generally officers of superior ability. Indeed, through ability, many good corps leaders earned army command, among them Meade, Sherman, and Philip H. Sheridan. Yet other corps commanders did not survive to receive promotion, for bullets respected no office. Jesse Reno, Joseph Mansfield, John Reynolds, and John Sedgwick were killed leading corps in battle.

Mortality among Confederate corps commanders was even higher: Stonewall Jackson, Thomas Green, Jeb Stuart, Leonidas Polk, A. P. Hill. Ability among Southerners was also higher for early corps commanders, like Jackson, Longstreet, Hardee, and Kirby Smith. Such ability soon peaked, however, for only Jackson demonstrated aptitude for still higher army command. The others proved disappointing at army level. Their replacements, moreover, often had difficulty even making the great leap from the technical expertise of tactics to the command latitude of grand tactics. Sound division commanders like A. P. Hill, Anderson, and Ewell failed to measure up as corps leaders. Of later corps commanders, only Forrest, Hampton, Gordon, and Richard Taylor really shined. Whereas the North progressively raised better officers from brigade to division and corps command, the South did not sustain the high quality of early leadership. Not only in manpower but also in command ability, Butternut resources ran low by war's end.

Most corps were mobile units of grand tactical and strategic maneuver. Some, however, were territorial commands for protecting geographical areas. The Confederate I Corps (West Louisiana), II Corps (Arkansas), and III Corps (Texas) each controlled a district within the Trans-Mississippi Department/Army. More often, those territorial corps were really small armies of independent departments, like the X Corps (Department of the South). And some were just garrisons, like the VIII Corps (Middle Department), with few mobile field forces.

Responsibility for territorial command rested at department level, and each department usually had its own army. Almost invariably, the department commander was the army commander. Early in the war, an army consisted of several divisions, but by late 1862 most armies contained several infantry corps or "wings," plus a cavalry division (later corps). Gray armies usually had three to five corps, while Blue armies had five to nine. Supporting engineer, provost, and signal troops also reported to army headquarters; and it was to armies that independent quartermaster and commissary departments delivered supplies.

Such broad control underscored the army's mission as the principal force for waging war. It defended its territory and invaded enemy territory. It conducted strategic maneuvers to apply overall force to military advantage, and it initiated or received battle. Once battle began, though, prevailing command principles left responsibility to chief subordinates. Much more than the army commander himself, corps and division commanders wielded the brigades that actually fought battles.

Federal armies and departments customarily were named for nearby rivers or bodies of water, whereas Secessionist armies and departments drew names from their geographic areas. Even when remote from their namesakes, most armies kept their names. Of all armies, only the Army of the Potomac had no department, yet the need to protect Washington and cover the North constrained it quite as if it had a fixed territory.

Sometimes strategic territory was so vast or the need to coordinate force was so great that no one army or department sufficed. To provide theater command, military divisions controlled several adjoining departments. Both sides created such structures, but Federal will and manpower put them to better use, especially in the region between the Appalachians and the Mississippi. There, under Henry Halleck, Grant, and Sherman, enough manpower existed to create a group of armies, each targeting a specific goal: the capture of Corinth, of Chattanooga, of Atlanta. Subsequently, Grant essentially continued that approach of directing several armies, against Richmond and Petersburg.

By then, he was general in chief of all Federal armies, the first such officer actually to take the field. Of his predecessors, Halleck remained in Washington; George McClellan was relieved just as active campaigning started; and Scott, who retired in 1861, was too old for field duty. Whether in Washington or the field, the general in chief was expected to coordinate all land forces, but again only Grant did so successfully.

The Secessionists had no real counterpart. R. E. Lee served briefly as general in chief in 1862 but was not reappointed until

February 1865, too late to do much good. His predecessor, the discredited Braxton Bragg, was more military adviser to President Davis than commander, and no one even nominally filled that office from June 1862 through February 1864. West Point–educated Davis reserved to himself overall conduct of the war.

The president greatly respected one of his best appointees, Lee. The great Virginian — with his audaciousness, tactical skill, and strategic vision — more than any other man, gave substance to Southern efforts for independence. However, other of Davis's choices, like John C. Pemberton, Holmes, and particularly Bragg, proved disappointing. With misguided loyalty, Davis retained them in command far too long. Presidential preference could not save Hood, whose disastrous army command lasted only six months, nor could it save Albert Sidney Johnston from a Yankee bullet — the only Southern army leader killed in battle. Still other army commanders, Beauregard and Joseph Johnson, killed themselves off feuding with Richmond instead of fighting Bluecoats. Above the pettiness and ineptitude towers Lee, but even he could not preserve the Confederacy single-handedly.

Neglecting able officers and retaining inept ones hardly characterized Davis's counterpart. Lincoln, if anything, gave officers too little time to succeed at army level. Turnover was high, and death accounts for little of it: only Nathaniel Lyon and James McPherson. Politics, irascibility, rivalry, overcaution, promotion beyond ability, occasionally even ineptitude more often proved the undoing of Union army commanders: McClellan, John Pope, Ambrose E. Burnside, Hooker, Don Carlos Buell, Rosecrans, Curtis, Banks, Butler, and Franz Sigel. But that terrible turnover, costly in lives and time, did create vacancies to which men who succeeded at lower levels could rise. Grant, Sherman, Meade, Thomas, Sheridan, Ord, and John M. Schofield ascended to army, theater, even overall command, and these were the generals who would win the Civil War.

Theater and army, corps and division, brigade and regiment — this was the command structure of the Federal and Confederate armies: the system for mobilizing, organizing, and wielding force to military advantage. But it was only a structure. It came alive, fell short, achieved success, prolonged the struggle, won the war according to the character and competence, weaknesses and strengths of the officers assigned to those commands — for they were the men who led.

For the Union, it was tragic from the first that one of her most capable soldiers was also one of her oldest. Lt. Gen. Winfield Scott was seventy-four years old at the outbreak of the war, yet still he would leave his mark on the prosecution of the conflict. Had he been ten years younger, he might still have led in the field. (USAMHI)

Alas, with Scott too old, and too few other generals available, the Union had to look in many directions to find leaders. For Lincoln, it would take years of trial and error before he found the right ones. For over a year he tried Maj. Gen. George B. McClellan, a favorite with his soldiers, but a man afraid to use them in battle. (USAMHI)

More would follow McClellan, among them his friend Ambrose Burnside. Reluctant to accept command of the Army of the Potomac until forced to, he proved a disaster. His lasting legacies were his dreadful losses at Fredericksburg and his name, forever tied to the sideburns that he wore. (USAMHI)

Some became early heroes without ever firing a shot or hearing a bullet whine. Maj. Gen. John A. Dix had been a politician, and U.S. secretary of the treasury just before Fort Sumter. When he told a subordinate in New Orleans, "If anyone attempts to haul down the American flag, shoot him on the spot," he was rewarded with a general's stars. (LC)

There were others whose careers seemed to have prepared them for command, men of the stripe of Maj. Gen. Henry W. Halleck. He would be a disaster in the field, but an able chief of staff. (VM)

Maj. Gen. Thomas Crittenden came from an important and influential Kentucky family, and it was politically expedient to elevate him to high command. He would not, in the end, prove to be up to it. (KHS)

Indeed, the early — and continued — Union habit of giving high commands to politicians proved almost invariably unfortunate. Maj. Gen. Franz Sigel helped mightily with enlisting thousands of fellow German immigrants. In the field he was almost incompetent. (USAMHI)

And Maj. Gen. Benjamin F. Butler was little better, yet so influential that he retained his command almost until the end of the war. (SC)

Top left: Others were better, if only marginally. Abner Doubleday never invented baseball, as legend says, but he helped defend Fort Sumter at the war's start, and that won him a generalship, and eventually command of a corps, though he never shone again as brightly as he had when firing the first gun to reply to Charleston's batteries that April 12, 1861. (WRHS)

Top right: Some of the politicos showed real promise in command. John A. Logan had been an ardent opponent of Lincoln's in the election of 1860, but he stood unswervingly for the Union in 1861. Made a colonel out of political expedient, he quickly rose through ability, and in time commanded the XV Corps and even, briefly, the Army of the Tennessee. (USAMHI)

Bottom left: Men who lacked the connections of Butler or the flamboyance of Doubleday still climbed high on their own merits, and few more so than Andrew A. Humphreys, who rose to corps command in the Army of the Potomac and, for a time, was chief of staff to its commander. (WLM)

Leadership could be at times a matter of flair and youthful exuberance, as much as ability. That George A. Custer possessed all three few would deny. Seated here at left, with Maj. Gen. Alfred Pleasonton, commander of the Cavalry Corps of the Army of the Potomac, Custer would shine as bright as any star in this war. His radiance would endure long after his flame was extinguished at the Little Big Horn in 1876. (USAMHI)

Flamboyance could be contagious. Many of Custer's officers affected his dress, and scores of other Federal leaders — like this man, identified only as "General Brayman" — showed an affinity for his flowing locks. (KHS)

A few of the Union's leaders were heroes of another war: the one with Mexico from 1846 to 1848. George Washington Morgan had so conducted himself then as a colonel that he was given the brevet—largely honorary—rank of brigadier, the youngest man in that war to receive such a promotion. In the Civil War, too, he would rise, eventually commanding the XIII Corps. (KHS)

And then there were the young, men like Adelbert Ames of Maine. A brigadier general at twenty-eight, his war career was distinguished from start to finish, yet ultimately he would be best known as the last survivor of all the generals of the Civil War. He died in 1933, aged ninety-eight. (SSC)

There were the undeniable greats. George Gordon Meade was the man who finally led the Army of the Potomac to major victory at Gettysburg, and thereafter he led it capably until the end. (KA)

Maj. Gen. Philip H. Sheridan became the Union's most ruthless and trusted cavalryman. Short, stocky, pugnacious, he stands here at center surrounded by other names legendary among Yankee horsemen. James H. Wilson sits at right; Alfred T. A. Torbert stands next to him, in Custer-style garb. Wesley Merritt sits at center, destined to become one of America's most distinguished soldiers. David M. Gregg sits at left, with Thomas Davies standing beside him. They were undefeatable. (MHS)

And, of course, there was Sherman — he who could make war hell, who split the South, took Atlanta, marched to the sea, and enjoyed the unswerving trust and confidence of his friend and commander . . . (NA)

U. S. Grant — the Union's essential soldier. Here he appears as he did early in the war, when just given his first general's star, and with the triumphs of Vicksburg and Chattanooga — and Appomattox — in the future. (USAMHI)

Across the lines there was talent aplenty, as well, some of it destined to become legendary. No soldier in American history, even Grant, would enjoy the aura of greatness that surrounds Robert E. Lee, shown here after the surrender on his war-horse Traveler. Grant was a soldier of the future; Lee was a soldier of the past, and of all time. (USAMHI)

Top left: High command went to Braxton Bragg, who should have been a great general but proved instead to be contentious, inept, frequently unstable, and perennially controversial. Yet for almost two years the Confederacy's major army west of the Appalachians would suffer under his leadership. (CHS)

Top right: Lt. Gen. Richard Taylor was the son of a U.S. president as well as a general, Zachary Taylor, and rose from an obscure colonelcy to a high position in the Confederacy. At the end, he would be the last general east of the Mississippi to surrender his army. (ADAH)

Bottom right: Contention seemed to infect Confederate leadership from the first, impeding the undeniable talents of generals like Pierre G. T. Beauregard, the hero of Fort Sumter and First Bull Run. This postwar portrait shows a proud officer who all too seldom saw merit in the ideas of others. (KHS)

Almost as difficult, though formidable when fighting in harness under Lee, was Lee's old war-horse Lt. Gen. James Longstreet. He appears as a brigadier here, sometime in the summer of 1861. He would outlive all the other high-ranking generals of the Confederacy. (LFH)

The South, too, had its gifted amateurs — surely none more talented than John B. Gordon of Georgia. He began the war as a captain, and ended it a major general and corps commander. No one compiled a finer record as a combat leader. (NA)

And there were men of principle, men like Simon Bolivar Buckner of Kentucky. At war's outset, both sides offered him a general's commission. Only when he had exhausted every effort on behalf of his state's attempt to stay neutral did he cast his lot with the Confederacy, ultimately rising to lieutenant general. He would survive the war by nearly fifty years, honored North and South. (KHS)

The haunting eyes of John Bell Hood bespeak a leader who felt the war's tragedy as few others. It cost him a leg, ruined an arm, saw him rise to the rank of full general, only to waste his army's blood at Atlanta and again at Franklin and Nashville. Like so many after the war, he would spend his remaining years arguing, trying to write and win with the pen what his sword had lost. (WRHS)

Those who did not fall in battle risked the monotony of capture and imprisonment. Here a host of officers, most of them Kentucky cavalrymen, pose in Fort Delaware prison, outside Philadelphia. Seated third from left is Brig. Gen. Robert B. Vance. Standing second from right is Basil W. Duke; as a brigadier, he would take over the slain John Morgan's cavalry after being released from prison. (USAMHI)

One captured Confederate general, William N. R. Beall, was even put to work for his fellow prisoners. Given his parole for not trying to escape, he was released to open an office in New York City where he sold Southern cotton to raise money to clothe and feed Rebel prisoners. (KHS)

For all of those who led, there was more than glory: there was risk and danger. For a few risk lay in their own foolishness, as with Confederate major general Earl Van Dorn, a dashing and able cavalryman who was killed in the end not by a Yankee bullet, but by a jealous husband. A previously unpublished portrait of the flamboyant Van Dorn. (ADAH)

Even more dashing was the inimitable John Hunt Morgan of Kentucky, Rebel raider without equal. Hunted down by his enemies, he was killed in his nightshirt on September 4, 1864. (KHS)

The Yankees had their casualties, too. Brig. Gen. Robert Nugent suffered his wound while leading his regiment, the fighting Irish of the New York Sixty-ninth. (USAMHI)

Brig. Gen. James S. Jackson of Kentucky was wearing the Union blue when he defended his native state against an invasion, and at the Battle of Perryville, Kentucky, on October 8, 1862, he was killed instantly by a bullet. (KHS)

James Mulligan was another one who died. At Winchester in Virginia's Shenandoah Valley, he was wounded and being carried from the field when he saw his regiment's flag about to be captured. "Lay me down and serve the flag!" he shouted. His men did as bidden, and he was taken instead, dying a few days later. (USAMHI)

And Maj. Gen. John Sedgwick, beloved commander of the Union VI Corps, exclaimed during the Battle of Spotsylvania on May 9, 1864, that the enemy "couldn't hit an elephant at this distance." Moments later he fell dead with a bullet in his brain. (KA)

Whoever they were, these men who led, they were serious at their work. Officers of the Ninth Michigan, their colonel seated at left behind the table, pose at the headquarters of the Army of the Cumberland at Chattanooga in February 1864. Atlanta and the battles for it lie ahead of them. (USAMHI)

By contrast, the tranquility of the tent of A. J. Hill, adjutant for the Third New Hampshire at Hilton Head, South Carolina, almost belies the fact that there is a war going on at all. (USAMHI)

The leaders were not all generals, and the men who led the men in the ranks took themselves very seriously indeed. Here, just two weeks after the Battle of Fredericksburg, the officers of the 153d Pennsylvania stand to have their tintype made. (USAMHI)

Folded arms gave an air of calm authority to Lt. George Myrick of Company E, Fifth Massachusetts. (USAMHI)

To be sure, they liked the individual portrait the best. Capt. Archibald McClure Bush of the Ninety-fifth New York. (USAMHI)

Arms could be folded south of Mason and Dixon's line, too. Maj. J. J. Lucas, CSA. (USAMHI)

And every leader had to make at least one try at the Napoleonic hand in the blouse. This unknown Rebel officer is no exception. (KHS)

Three officers of the Seventeenth United States Infantry try a casual pose in their greatcoats . . . (USAMHI)

. . . while four officers of the Seventeenth Michigan appear even more casual, walking sticks in hand. Yet Lt. Col. Edmund Rice, at left, has already made a daring prison escape in this war. (USAMHI)

Seven officers stationed in New Bern, North Carolina, share a news sheet for the camera. (USAMHI)

No leader could resist a pose at a scenic spot like the summit of Lookout Mountain. Generals and privates alike came here to stand above the clouds. (USAMHI)

Col. John E. Mulford of the Third New York was able to pose by a greenhouse in captured Richmond at war's end. (USAMHI)

The seated group with the Stars and Stripes in the background was an ever-popular pose, as demonstrated by these officers of the Twenty-second Massachusetts at Beverly Ford, Virginia. (USAMHI)

The men who led were served by the officers of their staff, and staff work rose to its own in this war. Grant enjoyed one of the finest staffs of anyone — many of them seated here, including Col. Ely S. Parker, an Indian officer seated second from left. (USAMHI)

Most of these young officers were attached to McClellan's staff in the fall of 1862. McClellan, and dashing leaders like him, could always attract the best and brightest young men to run their headquarters. The luster of the commander often rubbed off onto them, or so they hoped. (USAMHI)

No general was happy without a photograph of himself with his trusted staff. Brig. Gen. William S. Rosecrans sits second from the right, wearing a cape. (NA)

Maj. Gen. Horatio G. Wright sits in the doorway of an arboreal camp building, with his officers to either side. (USAMHI)

Brig. Gen. J. J. Abercrombie chose to sit in a chair in front of his headquarters, his staff behind him and a band ready at the side. (USAMHI)

Brig. Gen. E. V. Sumner acted less aloof, standing toe to toe with his staff, including his son at his elbow. (USAMHI)

No one was more devoted to the men who helped him lead than Maj. Gen. Joseph ("Fighting Joe") Hooker. Standing tall at center, he posed with them in Virginia when he commanded the Army of the Potomac. (USAMHI)

And when he went out west, he posed with them atop Lookout Mountain. (USAMHI)

Top left: Yet staged poses were not the way in which the soldiers in the ranks remembered the men who led them to battle, to victory or defeat. They remembered them in their headquarters in garrison, as here, in New Bern, North Carolina. (USAMHI)

Top right: They remembered them deep in the South, fighting to take the Rebel cities—as Maj. Gen. Quincy Gillmore, from his headquarters here at Hilton Head, fought to take much of South Carolina. (USAMHI)

And most of all, the soldiers remembered their generals out in the field at the end of the day's march, with orders to give, letters to write, and the wagons ready to hit the road again in the morning. Gen. George H. Thomas's headquarters of the Army of the Cumberland near Cassville, Georgia, in mid-May 1864. They are on their way to Atlanta. (USAMHI)

Comrades

A Story of Lasting Friendships

★

Albert Castel

IN ONE SENSE the typical Civil War soldier, Northerner or Southerner, never left home. More often than not the volunteer who answered the summons of the drums in the spring of 1861 joined an outfit — company, battery, regiment — made up in large part of men from his own locality and with whom he already had a greater or lesser acquaintance. Thus it was rather common for brothers and even fathers and sons to enlist together, for college students to switch from Latin drills to military drills under the command of one of their professors turned officer, and for most of the young men of a village and its vicinity to go off to war as a group. Later, when replacements were needed to bolster thinned ranks, usually they came from the same communities that had supplied their predecessors.

Raising troops in this fashion had a terrible drawback: too often a few minutes of carnage in a single battle destroyed a regiment and so plunged whole towns and counties into mourning. On the other hand, it possessed several compensating advantages for the soldier himself. Unlike modern-day recruits, he did not go into service a stranger among strangers. Right from the start he had companions, possibly boyhood pals, who helped him cope with the psychological and emotional strain of being far from home for probably the first time in his life and of adjusting to army ways. Moreover, should he fall ill, which was far too likely, he could count on them to do their best to take care of him, visit him when possible in the hospital, and — at the worst — comfort him in his last moments. Finally and most important, being surrounded by friends profoundly influenced his conduct in battle. When going into combat, especially the first time, he feared death — but also feared disgracing himself before his comrades and having them report to the people back home that he had played the coward. And once actually engaged in battle, the sight of a friend being killed or mangled could infuriate him and cause him to fight fiercely for vengeance. Wrote one Yankee soldier following the Battle of Gaines' Mill, June 27, 1862:

> My two tent mates were wounded, and after that . . . I acted like a madman. . . . I snatched a gun from the hands of a man who was shot through the head, as he staggered and fell. At other times I

would have been horror-struck, and could not have moved, but then I jumped over dead men with as little feeling as I would over a log. The feeling that was uppermost in my mind was a desire to kill as many as I could. The loss of comrades maddened me.

Without question one of the main reasons Civil War soldiers generally displayed such tremendous courage, determination, and an ability to keep going despite hideous losses is that their common home ties fostered strong personal ties. For the same reason, their desertion rate, high as it sometimes was, would have been higher still had not so many of them felt as did a Johnny Reb from Tennessee, who informed his wife early in 1864: "I would hate to be a deserter and have to run from home. . . . I want to be among the list who can return free from disgrace that would sink not only me but wife and children . . . beneath the dignity of the best class of Tennesseans for all time to come."

Combat — Civil War soldiers called it "seeing the elephant" — itself strengthened the sense of comradeship. Regardless of victory or defeat, if a particular unit fought well, its members developed great group pride and confidence. For example, as a result of their first engagement, in which they repulsed a larger enemy force, the men of the Twentieth Ohio, in the words of one of them, "acquired the belief that we were invincible in battle." Numerous other regiments in both armies felt the same way, as did Potomac's Iron Brigade; Cleburne's division, with it's unique "full moon" banner; and the XV Corps of Sherman's army, whose badge was a cartridge box inscribed with the figure 40. Soldiers belonging to these elite organizations possessed not only a high esprit de corps but a special relationship to each other that was a prime factor in their combat effectiveness.

Most of the time, however, the troops were not fighting but, in the words of one of their songs, "tenting on the old camp ground," occupied with the never-ending routine of drills, inspections, and, as one Indiana private put it, "wash, iron, scrub, bake — wash, iron, scrub, bake." In order to alleviate this daily drudgery, they organized "messes," usually numbering four to twelve men, who shared their food and the task of preparing it by taking turns making the fire, doing the cooking, and cleaning up. A mess also included, if it was not identical with, tentmates or those living in the same hut or other shelter.

At the beginning of the war, tents were large affairs, accommodating up to twenty men (as in the case of the Sibley model). Later, in the interest of greater mobility, the Union army issued each enlisted man a 5′2″-by-4′11″ canvas shelter half. By fastening their respective halves together by means of the buttons and buttonholes that lined three sides of the sheet, a couple of soldiers made a pup tent, which they suspended from a rope tied between two muskets stuck upright into the ground via their fixed bayonets. Normally, the men who paired off on this fashion already knew one another well; if not, they likely would become "the warmest of personal friends" in short order. The Confederates often lacked tents of any kind and so made do with only blankets, especially during active campaigning. But if the weather became too bitter and they had an opportunity, two or more of them likewise would band together to improvise a shelter out of branches, brush, or whatever else came to hand.

All through the war, in both armies, the existence of the average soldier revolved around his messmates and tentmates. It was with them that he played cards, went into town on leave, sometimes got drunk, conducted private foraging expeditions, discussed political and military affairs, shared boxes of food from home, marched the endless miles, and — when the time came — stood in the battle line. One of them, too, would be his particular "chum"or "pard," the comrade with whom, in the words of a poem of the day, he "drank from the same canteen":

There are bonds of all sorts in this world of ours,
Fetters of friendship and ties of flowers,
And true lover's knots, I ween,
The girl and the boy are bound by a kiss,
But there's never a bond, old friend, like this —
We have drank from the same canteen.

Religion both provided and promoted a different kind of comradeship. Men who think seriously about death are inclined to think seriously about God. Few did the former at the outset of the war — most assumed it would be over soon and took it for granted that they would live. But after seeing thousands of their fellows die, they began to realize that the same thing could happen to them — in fact, the chance of it happening increased with every battle. So more and more of them turned to religion and, in the process, to one another. Before the 1863 and 1864 campaigns, great revivals of the camp-meeting variety took place, notably in the Confederate armies. Writing from Dalton, Georgia, on the eve of the Atlanta campaign, one young Southern soldier reported to his sister: "I have never seen such a spirit as there is now in the army. Religion is the theme. Everywhere, you hear around the campfires at night the sweet songs of Zion. This spirit pervades the army."

Of course, once the fighting resumed, many a soldier who had "seen the light" quickly slid back into darkness: living and killing like wild beasts tend to have that effect. Yet in most regiments, Union as well as Confederate, there were at least some men who attended Sunday services if they could or met together to pray and discuss the Bible. Such soldiers, however few in number, possessed a relationship that went beyond the normal camaraderie of the camp.

When the "boys of '61" marched off to war, they expected to come marching back in a few months, victorious and glorious. Obviously, it did not work out that way. Instead the war went on and on, as did all of its tedium and misery and horror. Consequently, despite the good friends and occasional good times of the army, the strongest desire, the fondest dream, of the average soldier came to be getting a furlough to go home. Furloughs, however, were hard to get. Not until the winter of 1863/64 did either army grant them in large numbers, and in the case of the North it was done to induce the veteran troops to reenlist (if they did not, they would not be allowed to go home until their term of service expired — supposing they lived that long).

After receiving a furlough, the soldier headed home joyfully and was greeted the same way. But then something strange happened to many of them, particularly single men. Although everybody was nice and did everything possible to make their stay pleasant, they began to experience, as one Illinoisan confessed, an "uneasiness at home, a feeling of being in 'hot water.'" They discovered that they no longer had much in common with old friends, that they missed their army comrades, and that they even had an "eager longing for the hardtack and army rations of the front." When the time came to return to the army, they were secretly glad, and when they got back, some declared that they wished that they had not gone home at all.

This reaction is easily explained. The soldiers had undergone ordeals and formed associations that set them apart from civilians. Indeed, in certain ways they now had more in common with the enemy across the front than with friends back home. After all, *he* knew what it was like to be shot at, to march all day in the mud, and to try to sleep at night in pelting rain. Ever more frequently, as the war dragged on and when opposing lines were close and there was a lull in the fighting, troops on both sides arranged informal truces, then met to chat and trade Rebel tobacco for Yankee coffee. On occasion some of them visited the enemy's trenches or spent the night in his camp, and there were several instances of Federals attending parties behind Confederate lines! Needless to say, the generals frowned on such fraternization and issued strict orders against it. Hence, whenever it occurred, each side posted lookouts to give warning if a high-ranking officer approached. In that case the soldiers scrambled back to their respective positions, sometimes shouting to the men with whom they had been visiting, "If I have to shoot at you, I hope I miss." When not busy trying to kill each other, Billy Yank and Johnny Reb rather liked each other.

In the spring of 1865, the drums stopped beating. In small groups or alone the defeated men of the South made their way home, often wondering if it still existed. The triumphant men of the North proceeded by regiments and batteries to various army camps, where they turned in their weapons and obtained their discharges. Victor or vanquished, they all knew that they had taken part in a great adventure, that they had made history, and that it was unlikely they ever again would be involved in something both so awful and so awesome. "Ours," declared one of them later, "is a generation touched by fire." But what they cherished most was the comradeship forged in the heat of that fire; it was this that made the war something besides the hell that Sherman said it was.

One evening in February 1864, during a campaign in Mississippi, Maj. Benjamin F. Stephenson, surgeon of the Fourteenth Illinois, and Chaplain William J. Rutledge, of the same regiment, talked about what the troops would do when they left the army. Rutledge commented that "it would be but natural to suppose that men who had shared so much suffering, privation, and danger would wish to form some sort of association, that they might meet again to preserve the friendships and memories of the past." Stephenson agreed, and both promised to join in forming such an association after the war ended. As a result, they met again in Springfield, Illinois, in March 1866 and drew up the constitution and rituals for what they decided to call "The Grand Army Of The Republic," an organization open to all men who served in the United States Army, Navy, or Marine Corps between April 12, 1861, and April 9, 1865. The following month, the first GAR post came into being at Decatur, Illinois; on November 20, 1866, the first GAR national convention met in Indianapolis; and before long, GAR posts existed throughout the North and even in most Southern states.

In spite of this auspicious start, however, for a number of years the GAR contained only a small minority of Union veterans, mainly because of its close identification with the Republican party (Democrats charged that its initials really stood for "Grafting Army of the Republicans"). Not until the passion of Reconstruction-era politics cooled down and the GAR devoted itself to strictly nonpartisan (and highly successful) endeavors to increase veterans' benefits did it become truly representative of the former Federal soldier, ultimately achieving, in 1890, a peak membership of 409,484.

Other important Union veterans' organizations included the Military Order of the Loyal Legion of the United States, whose membership was restricted to officers and prominent civilian leaders; the Society of the Army of Tennessee, formed at Raleigh, North Carolina, on April 14, 1865, after news of Lee's surrender arrived; the Society of the Army of the Cumberland; and the Society of the Army of the Potomac. In addition, there were numerous more specialized or limited organizations, such as the Union Ex-Prisoners of War Association, the National Association of Naval Veterans of the United States, the Signal Corps Society, and the short-lived Colored Soldiers League (the GAR did not formally bar Negroes, but its posts were almost universally white). For many an old soldier, however, the most pleasant and meaningful association took the form of attending the reunions of his regiment or battery. Here he met his closest comrades of the war and with them could sit in "the bivouac of memory around the old campfire . . . and smoke our pipes together once again."

Confederate veterans made no attempt to establish a Southern-wide organization for a quarter of a century following Appomattox: the economic plight of the South made it impractical, and political considerations made it inadvisable. Apart from local and state associations, the only major organizations to emerge during that time were the Society of the Army of Northern Virginia, the Society of the Army of Tennessee, and the Veteran Confederate States Cavalry Association. Then, in June 1890, these three groups combined to form the United States Confederate Veterans at a convention in New Orleans. Filling a great emotional need, the UCV flourished; by 1900, it had chapters in every Southern state and several Northern ones as well, and its semi-official journal, the *Confederate Veteran*, had become a commercial success and a treasure trove for future historians (as are the publications of the Military Order of the Loyal Legion).

It was only a matter of time before Federals and Confederates began to do what they had done occasionally during the war — fraternize. In 1881, Union veterans from New York and Boston accepted an invitation to participate in New Orleans's Mardi Gras festival ("We of the South are anxious to show to you of the North that the war is over"). During the next six years, no less than two dozen formal Blue-Gray meetings took place, plus many more informal ones. The climax came July 1–3, 1888, when representatives of the Army of Northern Virginia joined old soldiers of the Army of the Potomac at

Gettysburg. Twenty-five years earlier these men had engaged in the greatest battle of the war; now they lined up on opposite sides of the stone fence that the Federals had defended and the Confederates had tried to take during Pickett's charge and reached across it to shake hands. Similar Blue-Gray gatherings occurred at Fredericksburg, Antietam, Kenesaw Mountain, and — biggest of all — at the dedication of the Chickamauga and Chattanooga National Military Park, September 18–20, 1890, during which forty thousand Northern and Southern veterans met to reminisce about the old times that, with the passage of the years, seemed in so many ways to have been good times.

Well into the 1900s, the veterans' organizations remained strong and active. Then, inevitably, they began to decline — at first slowly, but soon, ever more rapidly. After World War I, the American Legion and the Veterans of Foreign Wars spoke for veterans when it came to political and pension matters. By the eve of World War II, the legions of young men who had marched to the beat of the drums between 1861 and 1865 were reduced to a few thousand relics — treated, to be sure, with great veneration, but also apt to be regarded as curiosities. In 1949 the GAR held its last convention, and two years later so did the UCV; in each instance only a pathetic handful of members attended. Neither organization, however, officially ceased to exist until the deaths of the last-known surviving Union and Confederate soldiers: Albert Woolson, former drummer boy with the First Minnesota Heavy Artillery, who died in Duluth on August 2, 1956, aged 109, and Walter W. Williams, allegedly a teenage member of Quantrill's guerrillas, who passed away at the age of 110 in Houston, Texas, on December 19, 1959.

In another generation, few Americans will be able to recall so much as seeing someone who fought in the Civil War. Nevertheless, the memory of the men who wore the blue and the gray will not die. They saw to this themselves, with the letters, diaries, and memoirs they wrote and that have been preserved, and through the photographs for which they posed. By these means, they transcend time and provide for people today and tomorrow comrades from the past.

Top left: The camaraderie that arose between the men in the ranks during the war would stay with them for the rest of their lives. (USAMHI)

Bottom left: High and low, officers and privates, theirs was a common bond of affection, nurtured in adversity and hardship, that only death could sever. (KHS)

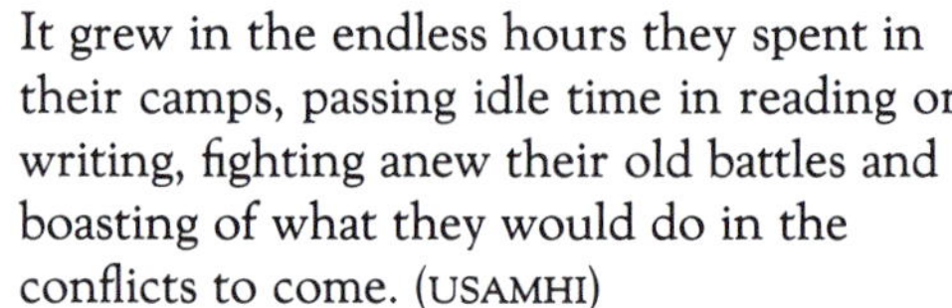

It grew in the endless hours they spent in their camps, passing idle time in reading or writing, fighting anew their old battles and boasting of what they would do in the conflicts to come. (USAMHI)

Everywhere the armies went the friendships grew—and in winter quarters like these most of all, for there was so little to do in the cold months that the men had to rely upon one another to pass the time. (USAMHI)

The bonds arose even as the first regiments volunteered — like the First Rhode Island, shown here in 1861. (USAMHI)

Across the lines it was the same. These Confederates of 1861, at their guns in Pensacola, Florida, would remember these days and their compatriots always. (USAMHI)

They loved to pose with each other for the camera, and were not ashamed to stand arm in arm. (USAMHI)

Of course, when they could, they had "man's best friend" with them as well. Men from Massachusetts and New Jersey units mingle for the cameraman. (USAMHI)

They played games, like these men of the Third New Hampshire seen at dominoes on Hilton Head in 1862. (USAMHI)

Bottom left: They made household items of the paraphernalia of war, even furnishings to decorate their spartan quarters. (USAMHI)

Bottom right: Those who could be visited by their children or friends shared them with their mates. (USAMHI)

And any visitor, even a top-hatted dandy, was a good excuse to dress up for the camera. Officers of the Second New York Heavy Artillery in 1865. (USAMHI)

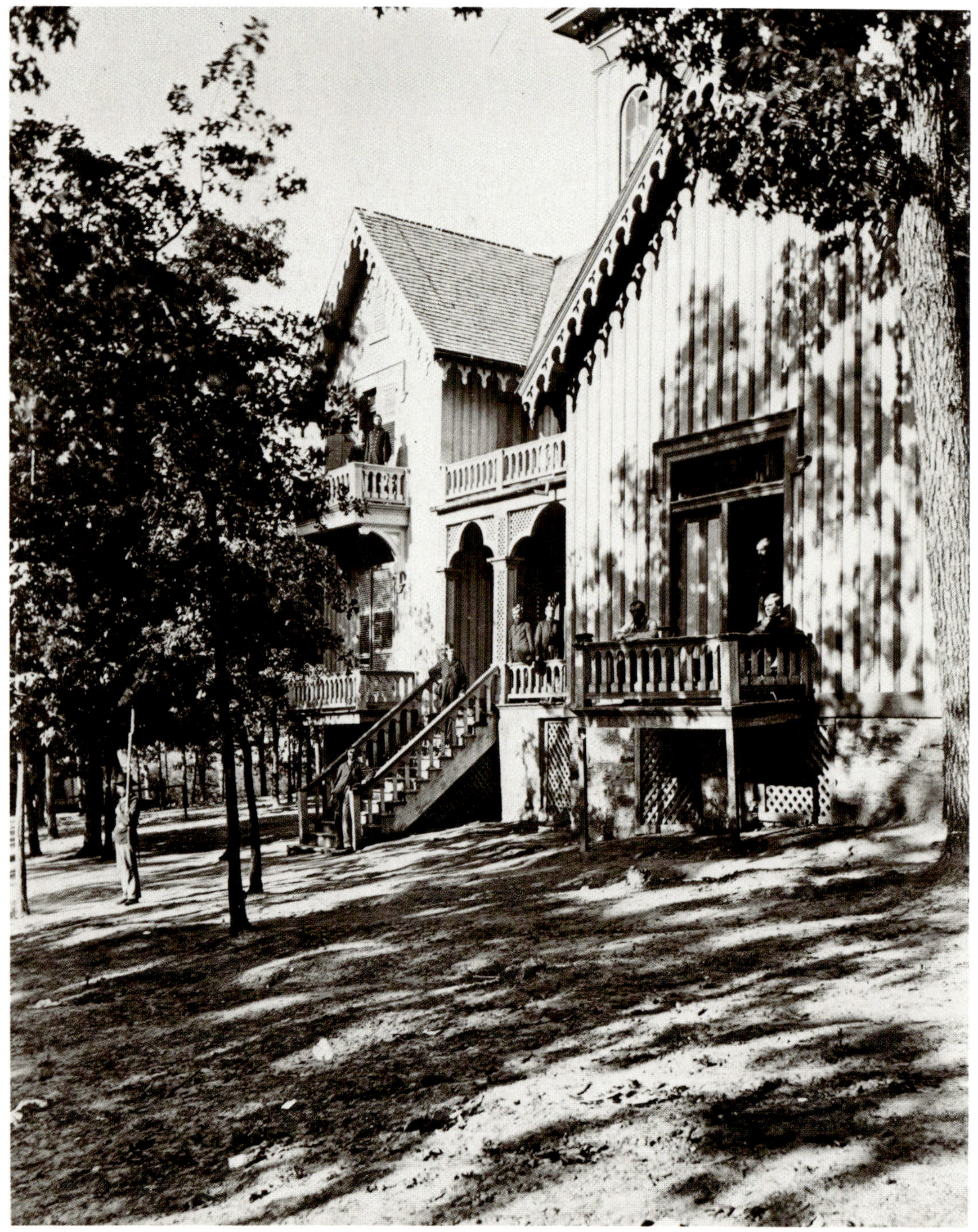

The fortunate might spend a few months in quarters like these atop Lookout Mountain. (USAMHI)

But most wintered in rude lodgings like these, somewhere in Virginia. With amenities all too few, and the winters cold, the men took comfort in their friendships with each other. (USAMHI)

They loved to clown and preen, whether just with an elongated cigar in the mouth, like the man seated at left, or by wearing what for all the world looks like a carpet. (USAMHI)

Soldiering seemed to involve an awful lot of sitting and standing around, as with these army scouts off duty at City Point, Virginia. (USAMHI)

A local store was always good for some kind of diversion — a new book, newspapers, perhaps a cake or pie to supplement the day's rations. Atwood's store on Hilton Head, in 1863. (USAMHI)

Fyler's store in Beaufort, South Carolina, was always a popular spot for lounging Yankees to spend some spare hours together. (USAMHI)

The shade of some trees outside the Bank of North Carolina in New Bern was just as welcome. (USAMHI)

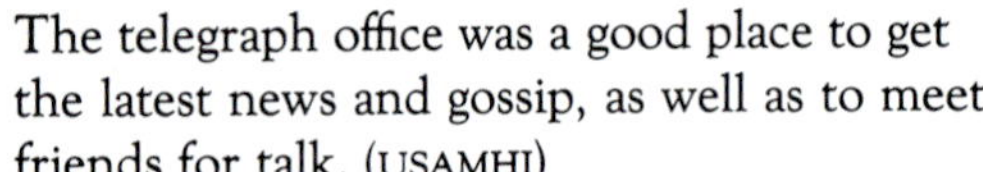

The telegraph office was a good place to get the latest news and gossip, as well as to meet friends for talk. (USAMHI)

The camaraderie was not restricted to the men in the ranks. The officers, too, like these resplendent leaders — the brothers D'Utassy of the Thirty-ninth New York — acquired a lifetime fondness for each other. (USAMHI)

But the greatest affection resided among the men in the ranks. Battery M of the Second U.S. Artillery at Culpeper, Virginia, in September 1863. (USAMHI)

Bottom left: Among the men on the water it was the same. Rarely would their contributions to the war be recognized for their worth, but no one ever undervalued the comradeship of men like these Mississippi River sailors aboard a tinclad. (USAMHI)

Bottom right: Like the old hymns they sang, their bonds of affection would last "till suns shall rise and set no more." Company F of the Forty-fourth Massachusetts, at Readville in September 1862. (USAMHI)

Very special ties of friendship grew in extreme adversity, and nowhere more so than among those who fell into enemy hands and languished in prison. These men, captured at the First Battle of Bull Run in July 1861, are confined in Charleston's Castle Pinckney. By later war standards, their accommodations are palatial. (USAMHI)

Indeed, even though prisoners of war, there is about them still an air of lightheartedness — they dubbed their quarters the "Musical Hall, 444 Broadway." (USAMHI)

These early prisoners, soon to be exchanged for Rebel captives and released, are the lucky ones. In years to come they may even look back on their captivity as a lark. (USAMHI)

For later prisoners it would not be so pleasant. There is already a different look in the eyes of these Confederates imprisoned at Maryland's Point Lookout. War has become harder now, and they need each other more than ever. (USAMHI)

Thousands of Rebels fill Chicago's Camp Douglas. Many will die here of disease and poor conditions. (USAMHI)

And worst of all, of course, would be Camp Sumter in Georgia, known to posterity simply as Andersonville. For thousands incarcerated in this living hell, only their friendships kept them alive. (USAMHI)

For those wounded in action, living through the days or even months in hospital similarly required the support of their comrades. Even in the better hospitals, like this one in Washington, D.C., recovery depended almost as much on luck and encouragement as on medicine. (USAMHI)

Only with death did friendships end, and even then the memories went on. In the foreground, the grave of a soldier drowned in the James River, near Fort Darling. (USAMHI)

With the war done, the comradeships went on, and not all of them between men. So closely did those who fought become that even pets — dogs and birds — and war-horses were beloved. Charlie, horse of the colonel of a Massachusetts regiment, was treasured for years afterward by the men of his regiment. (USAMHI)

In time, though happy with the peace, the men missed each other and began to meet again, this time for conviviality, old times' sake, and not war. Company B of the Thirteenth Massachusetts gathers at Nahant on July 9, 1876. (USAMHI)

The men of Knap's Pennsylvania battery and two other Keystone regiments enjoy a reunion on the field at Gettysburg where all of them bled years before. (USAMHI)

Amid tourists and onlookers, men who survived the hell of Andersonville gather again at Providence Spring, the trickle of water that miraculously appeared during a dry season in the war. (USAMHI)

At "The Weirs" in New Hampshire, members of the Grand Army of the Republic join in reunion. (USAMHI)

As the years went on, the veterans' ranks grew thin, and the reunions of "the boys" took on a look of age and depletion. Here, Company B of the Thirty-fifth Massachusetts meets at Andover in 1885. (USAMHI)

The same year, the more numerous Twenty-third Ohio meets at Lakeside, beneath its tattered banners. (USAMHI)

And the old men came back to the battlefields where they had spent their youth. These men of several Massachusetts regiments returned to Gettysburg twenty years after the battle, to stand with the monument to the Second Massachusetts. (USAMHI)

The generals joined the returning soldiers, themselves showing the ravages of the war, and time. Maj. Gen. Daniel Sickles lost his leg at Gettysburg. He never tired of returning to the field and seeing old comrades from the glory days. (USAMHI)

Veritable tourist excursions took veterans back to the scenes of their youth. A group of Yankees fill the steamer *Berkshire* more than twenty years after the war, on their way south to North Carolina, to the land where they spent their war service. (USAMHI)

There they could pause and look, and remember what they had done, and those who had not come back. One pensive Northerner stands on the bridge near Kinston, North Carolina, where two decades before there had been his war. (USAMHI)

Old-timers of the Forty-fourth and Forty-fifth Massachusetts look over the onetime site of Fort Washington near Kinston. It, like they, had eroded somewhat over the years. (USAMHI)

Yet there was still some of the gleam of old in their tired eyes, a brilliance that came from remembrance. (USAMHI)

Wherever the armies had gone, the veterans went back years later, as here at Hamilton Crossing, Virginia, where once Stonewall Jackson had battled. (USAMHI)

At Petersburg, in the great hole known ever after as the Crater, the fiery little Confederate general William Mahone stands front and center, leaning on his cane. In the war he had helped repulse Yankee attacks here. (USAMHI)

Fort Stedman, in the Petersburg fortifications, was almost overgrown twenty years later, but still the men came back. (USAMHI)

Wearing their veterans' badges, they gathered about their old leaders. In Lexington, Kentucky, in 1901, old Rebel cavalryman Joseph Wheeler stands at center surrounded by comrades from younger days. (KHS)

In addition to all this, the veterans tried to preserve the places that most reminded them of their years of comradeship, the places that held special meaning for them. There were the battlefields, to be sure. But there was also Providence Spring, where a chance appearance of water gave hope to thousands. (USAMHI)

Some of the more dedicated even began major collections of records to preserve the story of what they and their friends had done. Col. John P. Nicholson amassed one of the largest private libraries on the Civil War in existence. (USAMHI)

And the veterans with the money did even more. Here in Boston, for instance, members of the Military Order of the Loyal Legion of the United States erected this armory to preserve the relics of their youth. (USAMHI)

They built a massive library and collected artifacts from the war. (USAMHI)

Nothing was too insignificant to be worthy of preservation, nothing from the war was unimportant. (USAMHI)

And in these volumes they built the greatest collection of war photographs in existence. They still exist today, filling the books shown here with the scenes of young men's triumphs and hardships. (USAMHI)

In the end, their youth was gone. Like these aged veterans in the Kentucky Confederate Home, there was little left to them but the December of their lives. Yet it was for all of them a season filled with the memories of what they had done, what they had risked and won or lost together, touched by fire with their comrades. (KHS)

Contributors

ALBERT CASTEL has long been recognized as one of the leading historians of the Civil War in the West, thanks particularly to his outstanding biographies of Maj. Gen. Sterling Price and the Confederate raider William C. Quantrill. Professor of History at Western Michigan University, Dr. Castel is currently working on a major new history of the Atlanta campaign and the March to the Sea.

CHARLES EAST, formerly Director of the Louisiana State University Press and, later, the University of Georgia Press, is currently a free-lance writer living in Baton Rouge. His interest in Civil War photography, and particularly the work of A. D. Lytle, has already led to an excellent book on the wartime images made in Baton Rouge by Lytle and others.

ADM. ERNEST M. ELLER enjoyed a long and distinguished career in the United States Navy before his retirement. A natural outgrowth of his service is his avid interest in maritime history, as reflected in his works on the Civil War at sea and the Revolutionary War on the Chesapeake. For many years he has been an Advisor to the National Historical Society.

HERMAN HATTAWAY is Professor of History at the University of Missouri at Kansas City, and the coauthor (with Archer Jones) of the recent and widely acclaimed *How the North Won*, a study of Union strategy. In a forthcoming volume, he and his coauthors will deal with "How the South Lost." He is also the author of an award-winning biography of Gen. Stephen D. Lee.

PERRY D. JAMIESON is currently an Air Force historian assigned to the Strategic Air Command, though he is best known for his work on the Civil War, and particularly for his coauthorship of the controversial study of Confederate battle tactics *Attack and Die*.

RICHARD J. SOMMERS, Archivist at the U.S. Army Military History Institute, is one of today's foremost military historians of the Civil War. His award-winning book *Richmond Redeemed*, which deals with a phase of the Petersburg campaign, is a model study.

WILLIAM C. DAVIS, Editor of this work, is the author or editor of eighteen books dealing with the Civil War, including the six-volume *Image of War* photographic series. For many years editor of the magazine *Civil War Times Illustrated*, he now divides his time between writing and magazine management.

WILLIAM A. FRASSANITO, Photographic Consultant for *Touched by Fire*, is the leading Civil War photographic historian of our time, and the author of a brilliant trilogy dealing with the images of Antietam, Gettysburg, and the 1864–65 campaign in Virginia.

Photograph Credits

Abbreviations accompanying each image indicate the contributor. Full citations appear below. Very grateful acknowledgment is extended to the individuals and institutions, both public and private, who have so generously allowed the use of their priceless photographs.

ADAH	Alabama Department of Archives and History, Montgomery
CA	Cape Archives, Durban, Republic of South Africa
CHS	Chicago Historical Society
CM	Confederate Museum, New Orleans
DT	Donald Thorpe
FSU	State Photographic Archives, Strozier Library, Florida State University, Tallahassee
HP	Herb Peck, Jr.
IMP	International Museum of Photography, Rochester, N.Y.
JAH	John A. Hess
JM	Justin Martin
JPR	Jan P. Reifenberg
KA	Kean Archives, Philadelphia
KHS	Kentucky Historical Society, Frankfort
LC	Library of Congress, Washington, D.C.
LFH	Lee-Fendall House, Alexandria, Va.
MC	Museum of the Confederacy, Richmond, Va.
MHS	Minnesota Historical Society, Saint Paul
NA	National Archives, Washington, D.C.
NHC	Naval Historical Center, Washington, D.C.
NYHS	New-York Historical Society, New York City
OCHM	Old Court House Museum, Vicksburg, Miss.
PC	Private collection
PHS	Pensacola Historical Society, Pensacola, Fla.
RM	Robert McDonald
RP	Ronn Palm
SC/RSY	Sterling Chandler and Richard S. Young
SHC	Southern Historical Collection, University of North Carolina, Chapel Hill
SSC	Sophia Smith Collection, Smith College, Northampton, Mass.
TU	Tulane University, New Orleans
UR	University of Rochester, Rochester, N.Y.
USAMHI	U.S. Army Military History Institute, Carlisle Barracks, Pa.
VM	Valentine Museum, Richmond, Va.
WA	William Albaugh
WG	William Gladstone
WLI	Washington Light Infantry, Charleston, S.C.
WLM	War Library and Museum, Philadelphia
WRHS	Western Reserve Historical Society, Cleveland

Index

Page numbers in *italics* denote photographs of the subject. Unless otherwise indicated, italicized entries are vessels.